DEATH
IN THE
GARDEN

POISONOUS PLANTS & THEIR
USE THROUGHOUT HISTORY

DEATH
IN THE
GARDEN

POISONOUS PLANTS & THEIR
USE THROUGHOUT HISTORY

MICHAEL BROWN

WHITE OWL

First published in Great Britain in 2018 and reprinted in 2021 by
PEN & SWORD WHITE OWL
An imprint of
Pen & Sword Books Ltd
Yorkshire - Philadelphia

ISBN 9781526708380

Printed and bound by Replika Press Pvt. Ltd.

Pen & Sword Books Ltd incorporates the Imprints of Aviation, Atlas,
Family History, Fiction, Maritime, Military, Discovery, Politics, History,
Archaeology, Select, Wharncliffe Local History, Wharncliffe True Crime,
Military Classics, Wharncliffe Transport, Leo Cooper, The Praetorian Press,
Remember When, Seaforth Publishing and Frontline Publishing.
For a complete list of Pen & Sword titles please contact

PEN & SWORD BOOKS LTD
47 Church Street, Barnsley, South Yorkshire, S70 2AS, England
E-mail: enquiries@pen-and-sword.co.uk
Website: www.pen-and-sword.co.uk

Or
PEN AND SWORD BOOKS
1950 Lawrence Rd, Havertown, PA 19083, USA
E-mail: Uspen-and-sword@casematepublishers.com
Website: www.penandswordbooks.com

CONTENTS

Carnivorous Plants:

 DISCLAIMER: All the plants mentioned in this book can cause death or injury. The contents of this book are for interest only. The author and publisher accept no liabilty for any injury caused by the use of the plants.

INTRODUCTION

You may have picked up this book thinking that it is a murder mystery story. In some ways, you would be correct, because poisonous plants have played a major part in murders, passion and myth.

We imagine that gardens are a place of peacefulness, a refuge from the world, where we will be safe and escape the madness and dangers of the outside world; for the most part, this is true. But the garden has always had connotations of evil lurking within. God created the Garden of Eden and gave Adam the task of tending it. It was a place of beautiful trees and fruits that were good to eat, so whatever other people may say, gardening really is the oldest profession. To save him from becoming lonely, God created a partner from Adam's rib. Adam and Eve were happy in the garden until Eve was tempted by a serpent to eat of the forbidden fruit. She in turn tempted Adam and God threw them out of the Garden to henceforth earn their bread by the sweat of their brows.

Gardening became a way to stay alive for the majority of the population who had to grow their own food and that of their masters, but for the very wealthy it became a way to create their own paradise, a reminder of the lost haven of myth; yet the garden could become a prison and safety could be elusive. Some plants could make you very ill, or even kill you, if not used correctly. The fear of being bitten by snakes or other venomous beasts and insects is shown by the frequent antidotes provided by the early herbals. Murder and suicides are written about in stories and plays, which possibly reflected real life. Gardeners used poisons to kill the pests that attacked the plants that they needed for food, and in some cases the same poisons were responsible for the deaths of the gardeners too. Even today, many deaths and injuries are the result of tending to the garden.

A HISTORY OF POISONS

Plants generally seem to produce poisons to protect themselves, or parts of themselves, from predators that would eat them. Not every species is affected by specific poisons, and there is a wide range of effect within a species that consumes the poison.

As humans we may ask, 'What is a poison?' Paracelsus said that it is the dose alone that makes something a poison. He was correct, because the answer is not as straightforward as may be imagined. Many poisons have beneficial uses for both humans and animals – at the correct dosage. The problem does not end there, as what may be beneficial for some people, may affect others in a very different manner. Some people may be affected quite quickly with a dose of a poison, whereas others may only be affected to a lesser extent, or not affected at all.

The discovery of the practical uses of poisonous plants is now lost in history. How the poisonous properties were discovered and developed will probably never be known. The first discoveries are likely to have been accidental; the refining of their use is also not known, but presumably somebody had to experiment on somebody else, or did somebody make themselves ill, or die, by eating a new plant? Were prisoners of war or those who committed misdemeanours used for experimentation? Observation of wild creatures may have helped, but many species of animal may not be affected by the poisons in the same way as mankind. Many poisonous substances are quickly expelled from the body. The berries of most poisonous plants have a bitter or sharp taste that automatically makes you spit them out in disgust, but not all of them. Perhaps somebody ate the plant and was made ill. If they died then the conclusion was fairly obvious, but they may have survived, what then? Would they have described the effects to their companions who could then be more careful in future or make practical use of the plants properties? How anybody discovered that the roots of *Manihot esculenta*, Cassava, which contain cyanogenic glycosides, could be made edible is quite amazing. The pearl-like processed root was a staple food when I was a child; we knew it as tapioca.

The use of cassava possibly dates to 10,000 years ago in central Brazil, with the oldest proven growing of the plant for food 1,400 years ago at a Mayan site in El Salvador. In modern times, Africa is the country most reliant on the plant for food. The sweet tubers are the safest; the bitter ones can contain up to fifty times more cyanide and tubers collected during drought conditions are especially toxic. The pre-Columbian peoples of America make flour from the roots. When it is to be used, the flour is mixed with water to make a paste that is rolled thin, spread over a basket and left in the shade for five hours or more, when most of the cyanide will have broken down and the flour is safe to eat. The West African method is to put the tubers in water for a few days so that they begin to ferment and become soft. The peel and central fibres are removed and the remaining pulp pounded, then put in sacks and pressed with stones to remove the water, and with it the cyanide. Once pressed, the pulp can be dried thoroughly in the sun.

Poison has been used on arrow and spear heads from very ancient times, and continues in use for some cultures. Curare, the poison extracted from *Strychnos toxifera*, and blowpipes are synonymous, and were a mainstay of traveller's tales during the Victorian period, especially as the meat was still safe to eat. Poisons have been used to poison water and the fish within it, which is so much quicker, and easier, than fishing with a spear, bow, nets or line.

The fear of being murdered was constant for anybody with power throughout history. An assault of some kind is a very obvious way of removing somebody, but if you wanted to be subtler, poison was very useful. If the poison was administered carefully, perhaps nobody would ever know who the guilty person was. Poison has often been called the woman's method of murder, or even that of the less muscular male, but in reality, it was too effective to be not made use of by anyone with ambition. It could be slipped in to a medicine whilst the victim was ill and perhaps most people would believe that the victim had succumbed to their illness. The usual method was to add the poison to the food, so an intermediary could be employed as a sacrificial victim.

The position of food taster was a precarious existence. The food would need to be tested some hours before the person for whom it was intended would eat it, as many poisons were slow acting. Some toadstools, such as the Destroying Angel, *Amanita bisporigera*, could escape detection for days, and by then it is too late to save the victim. Hitler became paranoid about the risk of poisoning and kept food tasters; and even today President Putin apparently employs a food taster as a member of his security staff. Pliny recorded an antidote used by King Antiochus to counter not only assassination attempts using poison, but one that could be used against the bites of venomous beasts of all types. It became known as, *The Theracium of Antiochus*:

> 'Take two deniers of wild running thyme, Opoponax and Meu.
> Six deniers weight of the seeds of Dill, Fennel, Ameas and Parsley.
> Twelve deniers weight of Ervill flour.
> Beat all together into a powder, then add a little of the best wine and make into troches, each weighing half a denier.
> Dissolve a tablet in glass of wine and drink as required.'

I cannot see any ingredient in the list that would protect you from poisoning.

The person who seems to have perfected the art of surviving poisoning was Mithradates VI, King of Pontus during the first century BC. It is said that he took poisons in incremental doses in order to become resistant to them, in case an assassination attempt was made on him. His ploy was so successful, that when he did try to commit suicide using poison, nothing would work, so he had to ask a guard to kill him with a sword. Mithradates' recipe was alleged to have been found in his cabinet after his death and taken to Rome by Pompey. The recipe was reputed to have up to sixty-five ingredients. The antidote became so legendary that *Mithradate* became the word used to describe any antidote for poisoning. Yet once again, there was nothing in the recipe that would really help you if you were poisoned, nor prevent you catching the plague, as later writers claimed it would. One ingredient was rhubarb, which may possibly have emptied your bowels of toxins if it was taken in time. There is another option, that the medicine could have been part of a bluff to foil conspirators. If Mithradates was taking small doses of poisons to increase his resistance to them, it is more likely that it was this that helped to keep him alive. The story that he had a special medicine could have been a ploy to prevent people realising his real secret.

Pliny was certainly not impressed by the legendary power of the compound, and probably with good reason as most of the ingredients did not seem to be effective against poisoning and, except for rhubarb root, there isn't even a major purging plant.

Poisoners were feared in ancient times, firstly because it was easy to administer a poison, and secondly, it was difficult to do anything about it once you had been poisoned. A vomit or purge may work if given soon after ingesting the poison, but otherwise they would do little other than weaken the victim. Some poisoners became so notorious that we still remember them. The Romans certainly had good reason to remember

Locusta. She was probably born in Gaul, but that is all anybody knows of her until she was employed by the Empress Agrippina the Younger to help her to murder her husband, the Emperor Claudius. It is thought that she supplied a poison to mix in with a meal of mushrooms, so that the mushrooms would carry the blame. Claudius' food taster, Halotus, must have been involved as he does not seem to have been affected by the poison, and many people, then and now, have suspected that he was involved with the murder plot. Halotus was never punished for his alleged role and instead he gained wealth and status. Locusta also survived the scandal but was later convicted of another murder, but reprieved by the Emperor Nero, who then employed her himself to murder Claudius' son, Britannicus. Locusta was granted an estate by Nero and continued to prosper until Nero's death, when she was executed in Rome by the new Emperor, Galba. Sulla passed a law in 80 BC to make poisoning an offence. Henry VIII of England, passed a similar law in 1530, making poisoning as a wilful means of murder an act of treason; the punishment was to be boiled alive. The satirist Juvenal, writing in 1 BC, was one of many who noted that poisoning was used by many Romans, not only to remove unwanted spouses and step-children but the best way to receive an inheritance more speedily than waiting for the natural death of your father. Plant poisons that were available to Roman poisoners include Aconite, Colchicum, Hellebore, Hemlock, Henbane, Mandrake, Opium Poppy, Veratrum and Yew, although there were others that could possibly have been used.

Mostly dating from the Renaissance, Receipt Books, compiled by the lady of a wealthy family, have survived and can be referred to at local Records Offices. Many were passed on to successive generations, as they have been added to by other women at a later date. The receipt books contain medicines for man and beast, with others for food or more practical uses such as preventing rust on metal. Amongst the medicinal receipts there are usually several purging recipes, including wines, ales or beers that contain a purging ingredient. Distinction was made between downward purges and the upward purges, which were often referred to as *vomits*. Many purges for home medication were quite gentle. Lady Mildmay's receipts mostly used senna and rhubarb, rather than the more dangerous purges such as *Asarum* or *Daphne laureola*. Women have historically been the keepers of the household's medicine and poisons have been included in the cache. The Still Room, for distilling plant material, was also the woman's domain. Poisonous plants could be used to ease childbirth or abort an unwanted foetus. Toxic plants have been used to dull pain and to produce sleep. We still use opiates medicinally for this purpose. In the past, they may be used to relieve pain – perhaps permanently?

An inventory of Apethorpe House, dated 6 October 1691, listed the contents of the Still Room as:

'four cold stills and a limbeck (used for distillation), two tables, a stone mortar, a copper and worme and tub, a pair of bellows, a warming pan, two stools, two tables more, a little copper, one close stool and pan and two table leaves valued at £5.'

Another inventory of 3 November 1705 said that the Still Room contained:

'Three Stills, a Small Copper in brickwork, (similar to the coppers used for washing clothes that could be found in the shed, even in the early 1960s) two tables and two pair of bellows valued at £2-13s-0d.'

It also mentions that the Wash House contained a copper *Lymbeek and Worme* that were broken. Was the broken equipment the same as that mentioned in the previous inventory?

Poison rings have been shown in many old Hollywood films, where the baddie slips some poison from a ring into the intended victim's drink, or maybe they took the poison themselves to avoid torture. The rings certainly existed from around the sixteenth century, but were equally as likely to contain perfume, a lock of a loved one's hair or a holy relic; but that is not so exciting as being used to administer poison.

The detection of poisons is not always easy. It may be obvious that somebody has been poisoned, but a test must be carried out for each individual poison to decide which one has been used. This can be a lengthy and expensive process unless traces of the poison have already been discovered.

WITCHCRAFT AND POISONS

Witches were feared by the Romans as poisoners, sellers of drugs, love potions and spells. They were also consulted for their claims that they could converse with the dead, or other spirits, see visions and foretell the future. They were useful, but inspired fear, mistrust, suspicion and some respect. Christians were equally wary, especially as in Exodus 22, verse 18, it clearly stated; Thou shall not suffer a witch to live.

Witches were feared, but readily resorted to in times of need. The relief of pain invariably involved poisonous plants. The raging and relieving of human passions were equally likely to be resolved with toxic substances. Witches could usually provide something to help their customers. A sense of 'other worldliness' probably helped to create the sense of mystique and helped to ensure prompt payment.

The Romans equated witches and poisoning and shape changing, setting the tone for future outbreaks of alleged witchcraft. One of the earlier European references to witches flying is the Roman story of The *Golden Ass*, which is narrated by Lucius Apuleius, who wants to learn about witchcraft. He is told by his aunt that the wife of the man he is lodging with, is actually a witch. So, one day, Lucius secretly watches the witch as she rubs a magic ointment all over her body. Feathers begin to sprout; her nails turn to talons and her nose into a beak – and away she flies. Lucius tries to do the same but instead is turned into ass. He has numerous adventures before finally being turned back into a man.

By the height of the European witchcraft epidemic of the seventeenth century, witches were usually female, but not always. Looking like a witch was good enough to arouse suspicion, if not the certainty, of guilt. Reginald Scott described witches as being women who were old, lame, bleary-eyed, pale, foul, wrinkled, poor, sullen, superstitious and papists! Mistress Joan Flower, one of the Belvoir Witches, was said to have been:

> 'a monstrous malicious woman, full of oaths, curses and irreligious…
> her countenance was estranged and her eyes were fiery and hollow….
> so that the whole course of her life gave great suspicion she was a notorious witch.'

She was accused of being *Venecifici*, a poisoner or sorcerer, for dealing with poison and either killing or curing that way.

George Gifford mentions the use of poison by witches in his book, *A Dialogue Concerning Witches and Witchcrafts*, of 1593:

'A witch by the word of God ought to die the death, not because she killeth men, for that she cannot (unless it be those witches which kill by poyson, which either they receive from the divell, or hee teacheth them to make) but because she dealeth with divels. And so if a jurie doe finde proofe that she hath dealt with divels, they may and ought to finde them guiltie of witchcraft.'

In a sonnet that he wrote, addressed to Henry Boguet, the chief justice in France and one of its most notorious inquisitors during the late sixteenth century, Daniel Romanet mentioned the use of poisons by witches as *'Les charmes, les poisons...'* In his book about witches and witchcraft, *An Examen of Witches*, Henry Boguet recounted that when Francoise Secretain and Jacques Bocquet wanted to murder Loys Monneret, they had dusted some bread with a white powder. Similarly, when seeking revenge, Thievenne Paget mixed a white powder into a cheese that was to be eaten by Claude Roy and he died soon after eating it. Bouget believed that since the Devil would know the property of every herb, he could easily make a poison to kill man, woman or beast.

Boguet mentioned flying ointments used by the witches to attend the Sabbat. Some of the witches rubbed themselves with the ointment and were then carried away to the Sabbat, via the chimney. Yet it was not only the witches who could be transported in this way. Non-witches who had used such ointments were also taken away through the chimney, or had found themselves as far as one or two hundred leagues from home, and had difficulty finding their way home again.

POISONED CLOTHING

There are many stories of poisoned clothing. A gift of a glorious dress or a fine pair of gloves is given to the unsuspecting victim who gladly wears the clothes but then begins to feel ill, or as if their whole body is on fire, as the poison reacts to the moisture on their skin, before finally, they succumb to a horrible death.

In Greek mythology, Jason was married to the sorceress Medea who was descended from the gods; she had fallen in love with Jason during his quest for the Golden Fleece. Her father, King Aeëtes, said he would give Jason the Golden Fleece if he ploughed the field of Ares with the king's fire-snorting bulls. Jason would then have to sow the field with dragon's teeth, from which armed men would grow, whom Jason would then have to kill. Medea gave Jason an ointment to protect him from the bulls' fire and advised him to throw a stone into the group of men, who being argumentative warriors, thought that one of them had started a fight, and so they fought amongst themselves and were all killed. Jason did all that was asked of him, yet still Aeëtes refused to give Jason the Golden Fleece, so Medea made the dragon fall asleep, and Jason was able to fetch the fleece and, taking Medea with him, made his escape. Jason married Medea and they remained married for some time until Jason arranged to marry Glauce, the daughter of King Creon of Corinth. Creon wanted Medea sent into exile as he did not trust her. Jason told Medea he had no choice but to marry Glauce, as she was the daughter of a Greek king and Medea was only a barbarian, which in those days meant anybody who was not a Greek. Jason offered to keep Medea as his mistress and continue to support her, but Medea reminded him that it was she, a mere barbarian or not, who saved him and slew the dragon; but Jason would not change his mind. Medea went away and plotted her revenge. She took a golden robe that had been a gift from the sun god, Helios, and a gold coronet and very carefully rubbed poison into them. Medea then asked Jason for forgiveness for having argued with him and offered Jason the robe and coronet as a gift of friendship for Glauce. Jason accepted them and agreed that their children would take the presents to Glauce and Creon. Later, a messenger described what had happened. Glauce had put on the robe and coronet, but very soon she felt as if her body was on fire and screamed in agony. Her father had tried to save her, but he too was poisoned as he struggled to claw the robe from off his daughter, and they both died a painful death.

Medea decided to complete her revenge by killing the children that Jason was now prepared to abandon for his new wife. At first, she faltered, but then she grabbed a knife and murdered her own children to avenge herself on Jason. To rub salt into the wound, she made her departure in Helios' chariot with all the children's bodies, denying Jason even the chance to bury them and as she rode off, she cursed him to an awful doom.

Another myth tells how the lascivious centaur, Nessus, kidnapped Deianira, the wife of the ancient Greek super-hero, Hercules. Hercules found out and rushed off to rescue his wife, catching up with them as Nessus was carrying her across the river Euenos. Hercules took out his bow and an arrow he had poisoned with the blood of the Hydra that he had killed in an earlier adventure. He took careful aim and shot the centaur. The dying Nessus managed to carry Deianira to the far bank, where he collapsed on the ground in a pool of blood. As he lay dying, he told Deianira that if she saved some of his blood she could use it to make Hercules remain faithful to her. She secretly kept some of the blood hidden at home. Before he met Deianira, Hercules had once been in love with Iole, the daughter of king Eurytus of Oechalia, and had won the right to marry her by winning an archery contest, although in the end the king refused to allow the marriage. When Hercules once again pursued his love for Iole, the jealous Deianira took a potion made with the blood and poured it onto Hercules' lionskin robe. The blood still contained some of the poison that had killed the centaur and it took effect on Hercules. Immediately he writhed in agony as if his body was on fire. Eventually, to end his pain, Hercules threw himself onto a pyre on Mount Oeta and burned to death. When Deianira heard what had happened she became so distraught that she killed herself.

The Catholic queen of France, Catherine de Medici, was rumoured to have murdered the Protestant Jeanne d'Albret, by giving her a pair of poisoned gloves. Scented gloves were a popular gift amongst the wealthy. The leather gloves could be carefully soaked in perfumed oils until the desired strength of the scent was achieved. France was politically divided by faith and one way to heal the rift would be a marriage between Catherine's daughter, the Princess Marguerite and d'Albret's son, Henry. Negotiations were not going well and then, only two months before the proposed wedding, Jeanne d'Albret died unexpectedly. The discord between the two women was well-known and gossip soon spoke of murder using poisoned gloves. Modern research suggests that Jeanne d'Albret is more likely to have died a natural death from tuberculosis; and just how easy would it be to get a large enough dose of poison into an intended victim by using poisoned gloves?

The only factual poisoning from clothing occurred during the Victorian period, when Paris Green became the fashionable, must-have colour. The dye was made by mixing copper and arsenic trioxide, otherwise known as white arsenic. The regular handling of the dye was dangerous to those who worked with it and many became very ill or died. A ball gown could contain up to 900 grains of arsenic, and a headdress of artificial leaves held enough arsenic to kill twenty people.

The most famous family with a reputation for poisoning is the Borgias. The beautiful Lucrecia Borgia has possibly suffered from a bad reputation by association, but her brother Cesare probably does deserve the reputation that he has for murder and intrigue, whilst his father, who had become Pope Alexander VI, may have also been involved. By misfortune, or from deliberate intent, many of the Borgias' enemies seemed to have died in dubious circumstances. The Borgias are said to have used a poison known as Cantarella. The recipe is lost forever and died with the Cesare, but the main ingredient is thought to have been arsenic. The tables may have been turned on the Borgias during a meal hosted by Cardinal Adriano Castellesi, after which many of the guests later became ill. One person who died was Alexander, whose blackened and swollen body was reliably recorded. The rumours were of poison; others claim malaria or some other illness. Whether Cardinal Adriano Castellesi had discovered the plot and turned the tables on the Borgias, who knows? But it is hard not to see it as poetic justice.

Equally famous was the Affair of the Poisons at the court of Louis XIV at Versailles. In a court that thrived on licentiousness and intrigue the outcome was hardly surprising. The affair seems to have come to notice in 1675 following the trial of Madame de Brinvilliers who was accused of trying to poison her father, Antonine Dreux d'Aubray, in 1666 and two of her brothers, Antoine d'Aubray and François d'Aubray, in 1670, so that she could inherit their estates. The rumours were that she had perfected her poisons by experimenting on poor patients while she visited them in hospital. She fled to avoid arrest but was captured, tortured and confessed. She was sentenced to death and on 17 July 1675, she was beheaded, and her body burned at the stake. Her lover, the army captain, Sainte-Croix was lucky, having died of natural causes in 1672. Louis and many others were now fearful of the threat of poisoning. Accusations of aphrodisiacs, black masses, magic, poison and witchcraft rapidly spread throughout the court. Those at the fringe were arrested first; the alchemists, fortune tellers, magicians and dealers in potions. Many were tortured and confessed. Names were given. Those in the upper circles were now implicated. La Voisin, a midwife was accused and it was claimed the bones of many babies had been found in her garden, the alleged result of drugs used to induce abortions. La Voisin implicated the king's mistress, Madame de Montespan. La Voisin and many others were executed, having been found guilty of witchcraft and poisoning. Some of the accused were exiled, but to prevent the affair becoming too public, many of the accused were simply locked up in prison for the rest of their lives under the provision of a letter de cachet.

Life became more difficult for those using arsenic as a means of murder when, in 1836, James Marsh, a chemist, devised a reliable chemical test for arsenic. Marsh had been called as a witness in the trial of John Bodle, who was alleged to have murdered his grandfather with arsenic in his coffee. Marsh had used the standard test of the time for arsenic using hydrochloric acid and hydrogen sulphide. He succeeded in proving that arsenic was present, but by the time he got to court to show the jury the arsenic had deteriorated and Bodle was allowed to go free because of reasonable doubt. Marsh was inspired to invent a better test. His new method was so good that he was able to find one fiftieth of a milligram of arsenic.

THE PROPERTIES OF POISONOUS PLANTS

Medicine was not averse to using poisonous plants to alleviate pain, but some of the cures could be quite dangerous for the patient, especially purging and bleeding. Herbals often refer to plants being hot or dry or moist or wet, to degrees varying between one and four. One was the least potent, whilst four was the most powerful. This system was related to the theory of humours. The human body was thought to contain four liquids, known as humours, the most obvious one being blood. The other three were black bile, yellow bile, and phlegm. The humours were also related to other properties: the human temperament; the cardinal points of the compass; north, east, south and west; the stages of life; birth, youth, maturity and old age; the seasons of the year; spring, summer, autumn, winter; and degrees of heat and moistness.

These ideas led to a complex system that helped with both diagnosis and cure. The colour of the hair and the skin were also thought to be indicators of the dominant humour. The humours were indicative of the basic character of a person; the perfect human would have all the humours in their body in perfect balance.

In reality, this was impossible. Most people were not of a single archetypal humour, but a mixture, tending to be dominated by one or two humours, and if they became out of balance a person could become ill. The humours could be controlled by diet; so that a person who was too hot could eat cool food, such as lettuce, to bring down the heat. Depending on how out of balance somebody was, you could increase the medicine's effect by using more potent plants of four degrees. If diet and a moderate lifestyle were not having enough effect, then something more invasive may become necessary. Blood could be reduced by bleeding. Films and books usually show blood taken from a vein at the inside of the elbow, but there were diagrams to show different blood-letting points on the body to achieve different outcomes. The circulation of the blood was not known until it was proved by William Harvey, who published his, *Exercitatio Anatomica de Motu Cordis et Sanguinis in Animalibus,* in 1628; but bleeding continued to be used as a medical process even when the circulation of blood was fully understood. For the other three humours, purging could be used to bring them back into balance.

The purge could be upward, and was known as a vomit, to induce vomiting, not to prevent it. Downward purges promoted diarrhoea. Other purges induced urine or sweating. The most effective purges, by their very nature, tended to be toxic. Herbals say that some should only be given in incremental doses to avoid poisoning the patient. A safer way to give the purge to avoid the problem of orally ingesting the poison was to give an enema, using a clyster or glister pipe.

John Arderne, the fourteenth century surgeon who was a contemporary of Chaucer, gave detailed instructions on the making of the clyster pipe. A wooden tube should be made from box, hazel or willow. It was to be six or seven inches long and to be free of splinters and polished very smooth. A pig's bladder should be cleaned and then dried. A spoonful of salt, mixed with the same of water and honey was then put in the bladder for two days. Every day the

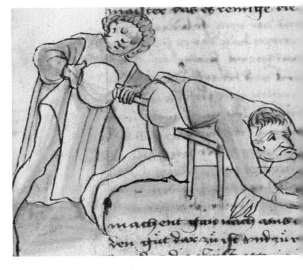

bladder should be shaken to ensure that the liquid is thoroughly soaked into the bladder. Then, the bladder should be emptied and blown up followed by binding the mouth so that it stayed inflated. It should then be hung in the shade until it is needed. No more than a pint of your herbal mixture should be put into the bladder, then tied to the clyster pipe, which was lubricated with pig's grease, butter, common oil or honey. The pipe was then inserted into the patient and accompanied by gently squeezing the bladder. A chamber pot should be close at hand. To keep a patient healthy, they could be purged twice in winter, once after Lent and again in summer; with other purging given as required. As can be seen from the expression on this patient's face, it was not a pleasant experience.

Syringes would later replace the pipe and bladder, but the contents of the medicines remained much the same and the use of a clyster, or glister, remained a standard medical procedure.

The Syon Herbal provided the recipe for an unguent that provoked vomiting;

'Take White Hellebore (Veratrum), Black Hellebore, Ramsons, Henbane, vinegar, Houseleek, White Bryony and mix them together with old grease. When required, rub the ointment onto the patient's hands and the feet.'

A very potent mixture indeed.

Bleeding and purging may have hastened the fate of many patients until well into the 1800s, without anybody speaking out against both practices. So, it seems surprising that Nicholas Culpepper, who was not a physician, had already spoken out against purging when he was writing about the uses of *Asarum*;

> 'The truth is, I fancy purging and vomiting medicines as little as any man breathing doth, for they weaken nature, nor shall ever advise them to be used, unless upon urgent necessity. If a physician be nature's servant, it is his duty to strengthen his mistress as much as he can, and weaken her as little as may be.'

The doctors continued to prescribe bleeding and purging for many years. George Washington would have probably died anyway, but the medical treatments used by his doctors would not have helped his condition; although he seems to have believed the theories himself and to have approved of what his doctors were doing to help him.

On the 12 December 1799, Washington rode around his estate to supervise work. The weather was cold, reported as being about 30°F (-1°C), and alternating between rain, hail and snow. He returned home and went to dinner without changing out of his wet clothing, despite having got wet during the day. The following day, ironically Friday 13, Washington supervised outdoor improvement work and he later developed a sore throat and a cold. The following day he complained of the ague and had trouble speaking and later of having difficulty breathing. First, he was bled at his own request and despite his wife Martha's concern, by George Rawlings who extracted twelve ounces of blood. This did not appear to have any curative effect. He was then given a drink of butter, molasses and vinegar to ease his sore throat, but he found it difficult to swallow and began choking so badly that he nearly died.

He was bled of a further eighteen ounces of blood at 9.30am and the same again at 11.00am. The family doctor, Dr James Craik, who was also a long-standing friend of Washington, eventually arrived. He produced a blistering of cantharides on Washington's throat, hoping to balance his humours. He then bled him again. Craik then asked that a gargle of sage tea and vinegar should be made. Things could not have been going well as

Martha asked that Dr Gustavus Brown should be sent for.

By 11am, Brown had still not arrived, so Craik sent for another doctor. At noon, Washington was given another enema and not long after he was bled for the fourth time; it was later said that on this last occasion alone, that thirty-two ounces of blood were taken. Later still Craik used another vomiting potion, which hardly surprisingly, had little positive effect and Washington's condition became worse. Dr Elisha Cullen Dick wanted to attempt a tracheotomy, but it was not a well-known medical procedure in America at the time, and the other two doctors objected.

Eventually Washington, having been weakened by the loss of about forty per cent of his blood and the several purges and blisterings that he received, died at some point between ten and eleven at night, on 14 December 1799. Since his death there have been many debates by doctors on the actual cause, but malpractice on the part of his doctors has been ruled out. Perhaps those who could not afford to pay a doctor were the lucky ones.

THE SPIRITUAL PROPERTIES
OF POISONOUS PLANTS

Religion has often made use of the toxic properties of plants to help its practitioners to converse with the gods or to induce prophetic visions. Each generation has its own drugs, whether it is tea, coffee, tobacco, alcohol, opiates, absinthe or cannabis. Some have become accepted by society, whilst others are objected to or become illegal. During the 1960s, writers such as Timothy Leary extolled the virtues of psychedelic drugs such as LSD to expand the mind. Having been sacked from Harvard University in 1963, Leary experimented with LSD with an ex-Harvard psychologist, Richard Alpert. They came to believe that their experiences were the same as those described by the Tibetan Book of the Dead, the *Bardo Thodol*, and published their findings in a book, *The Psychedelic Experience: A Manual Based on the Tibetan Book of the Dead*, in 1964. The book became very influential. Artists experimented with LSD and recorded their experiences in words, paintings and music.

LSD was first processed in 1938 by Albert Hoffmann, who extracted it from ergot, a fungus that grows mainly on the grains of the rye plant. During the medieval period, poisoning by ergot was usually the result of eating infected rye bread. The victims felt as if their limbs were painful, as if on fire, resulting in the symptoms being known as Saint Anthony's Fire. Other effects could be hallucinations, nausea, loss of strength and vomiting. The current belief in demons must have given many of the victims a sense of being attacked by the devil and his minions. Gangrene, leading to the loss of hands and feet, could occur, making outbreaks of ergotism something to be feared.

Governments wishing to restrict the use of drugs by banning them have found it difficult to keep up with the rate of the production of new drugs as alternatives were found that were not covered by legislation. This has led to the current trade in so called legal highs that have also caused numerous deaths. Most of these products have not been properly tested for adverse side effects, especially in the long term. The internet offers many sites dedicated to people who will try anything and risk their health and life for the promise of something more exciting than their usual humdrum daily life. I am sure there are sites whose products do contain the substances that they claim, but the quality cannot be guaranteed and there are unscrupulous dealers, many trading from abroad, against whom it will not be able to easy make a legal claim in the event of problems. I have seen dried mandrake root for sale for mystical purposes, but with no mention that it is poisonous.

Magic mushrooms became popular and can be often found on the front lawn or a nearby public park. I remember seeing students crossing the road from a local college to reach the park where magic mushrooms grew. Thankfully the mushroom is fairly easy to identify, so there have been few problems as a result from the actual ingesting of them.

Currently, there are many travel companies that organise shamanic tours for people who want to go to South America to drink local shamanic brews such as *Ayahuasca*, made from *Banisteriopsis caapi*; *Psychotria viridis*; *Diplopterys cabrerana* or *Tabernanthe iboga*; that it is claimed will induce spiritual and mystical experiences – and usually vomiting as well. This is hardly surprising, as most of the plants are toxic, which is why they cause visons as the brain is affected and the vomiting is the body's attempt to expel the poison. If you were to try the ceremony, you would need to be careful and have to trust that the people mixing the drugs know what they are doing, and what to do if something goes wrong. Some of the plants are being harvested in large amounts to cater for the growing market, with environmental worries about the decreasing number of wild plants, because some of the plants may have medical uses. In the past, people may have gained a certain amount of power as shamans, mystics, oracles and spiritual guides, but today they are often destitute and an object of scorn. There are safer ways to find enlightenment.

THE WRITERS ABOUT POISONOUS PLANTS

The early use of poisonous plants is usually hidden in medical books and herbals. The men who wrote the early herbals or books about plants, often had quite exciting lives. Most of them were doctors, for whom plants were the main source of medicines, and a mistake of identification could be fatal.

The ancient Greeks and Romans had recorded the use of plants from other cultures older than their own. As the Roman empire expanded across Europe and Asia, even more knowledge was gained and written down. Hippocras, sometimes called the Father of Medicine, was born on the Greek island of Cos. The collection of medical writings known as *Corpus Hippocraticum*, is likely to contain only a few of the works of Hippocras himself. It is possible that he compiled the collection or that later authors ascribed the collection to him in order to gain a respected authority for them. The ideas in the collection include very sound medical practice, such as assessing the age and bodily strength of the patient. The importance of diet was also stressed. This would remain an important aspect of later medieval health care.

Dioscorides was an Asiatic Greek who was a surgeon in the army of Emperor Nero. He wrote *De Materia Medica*, which describes around six hundred plants that had medicinal or practical use. The plant descriptions are often very brief, which made life difficult for scribes from northern Europe, who did not know the plants that he was describing, and it is still the cause of much debate today. He was still being referred to, and copied, in the seventeenth century by people such as Nicholas Culpepper.

Gaius Plinius, usually referred to as Pliny the Elder, c. AD 23-79, was a contemporary with Dioscorides. He wrote *Historia Naturalis*, his compendium on nature. This includes a series of books on the nature of trees and plants with their medical virtues. He was not very discerning about what he wrote, with the result that later generations continued to pass on the incredulous tales and the superstitions that he recorded. He has been accused of being gullible, but maybe he preferred to let his readers decide on the truth as they wished. His work was also copied without question by many future writers. Having said that, his notes on cultivating vines were very practical and probably based on what was actually taking place on his own estates.

Galen was born at Pergamum c. AD 129 and died in AD 200, although there is some argument about the exact date when he died. He studied surgery and practiced as a physician, possibly gaining practical experience at a school for gladiators. He became the physician to Emperor Marcus Aurelius. He dissected the bodies of animals and developed his own theories on the workings of the organs and the spinal cord. His writings were based on this research. In the centuries that followed, he was considered to be the definitive authority on anatomy, and his errors were repeated by subsequent authors without any checks on his work. It would be many more centuries before research corrected his mistakes. Following the fall of Rome, much of this knowledge was lost, or no longer widely available, except to the church.

The medieval authors of herbals and other books often showed a reverence for the golden age of the Roman period, much as the Romans had looked back to the Greek civilisation. Medieval scribes peered through rose tinted spectacles to a time when they believed Europe was a united whole and scientific knowledge was at its peak. The medieval writers initially compiled their own précis of earlier knowledge and took earlier herbals at face value, without questioning even the most obvious delusions and mistakes of previous writers.

There were other influences from outside Europe. As the Muslim invaders of Southern Europe became more settled, their scholars began to study and translate both Greek and Roman writings, often adding their own experience to the corpus of earlier knowledge. These volumes later became available to Christian society as the two conflicting cultures gradually began to trade, leading to an exchange of ideas and experience. The earliest English vernacular writings are found in the *Leech Book of Bald*, c. AD 900-950. It is mostly based on English native plants, with some classical references, but added more recent practice, especially the Christianising of earlier pagan charms. The first illustrated English book was the *Herbarium Apuleii Platonici*, c. AD 1000-1050.

A later book that became influential in Europe was written by Pietro de Crescenzi, a lawyer from Bologna. During his retirement, he wrote *Liber Ruralium Commodorum*, a book that drew on classical authors but which also referred to authors of the early medieval period, including Arabic writers such as Avicenne, or Ibn Sina, who had written two very influential books, *The Book of Healing* and *The Canon of Medicine*. The first book is scientific, but it was the second book that became important in medicine.

Crescenzi's book was essentially an up-to-date version of the early Roman books on how to run your estate, and followed the same format. His descriptions of medieval gardens and pleasure parks have been of great importance to garden historians, as little writing on gardening has survived from this time. He wrote chapters on the use of plants, quite a few of which are poisonous, and include instructions for their use or processing. The book remained important for centuries; even Henry VIII of England owned an illustrated copy.

John Arderne was a military surgeon, who may have begun with a classical training, but learned by experience and, unlike many men of the time, lived long enough to write down the things that he had learned. Little is known of Arderne's early life, but he was probably related to the Arderne family who were the Lords of Watford, Northamptonshire from 1140, later spreading to Cheshire and Staffordshire. John became a customary family name and one John Arderne was appointed as Seneschal of the Manor of Passenham, Northamptonshire in 1374. Which branch of the family John Arderne the surgeon was descended from is uncertain, but from his own writings we know that he was born in 1307. There is some evidence that Arderne may have studied at the medical school at Montpellier and been a surgeon during the Hundred Years War in France. Evidence suggests that Arderne served under Henry Plantagenet, the First Duke of Lancaster, who was at Antwerp in 1338, where Arderne is said to have practiced. Henry fought at the siege of Algeciras, and Arderne was also at Algeciras as he wrote of how he cured a knight there. Arderne never said that he had served under Henry, but he accurately wrote down the order of the towns that were visited during the campaign thirty years after the events. It is thought that he later served under John of Gaunt.

John Arderne was not one to rely on inherited wisdom. He worked within the beliefs of his time, but he experimented with new methods to solve his medical problems, and unlike some, he was not afraid to say when he failed. He wrote on many subjects, but his most famous and influential work was *Fistula in Ano*, where he described his tried and tested methods for removing a fistula, a painful lump that forms between the anus and the base of the spine, which was usually caused by spending long periods of time mounted on a horse back. The operation had been feared by previous surgeons because it was difficult and the period of recuperation for the patient was several months. Arderne did not invent an entirely new process, he refined it and made it much safer. He was not just a surgeon, and he recorded several plant-based recipes, using opiates and other poisons as sleeping draughts and painkillers and other plants to cure problems without using surgery.

Arderne became a Master of Surgery, making it clear that he was no common Barber Surgeon. In his writings, he gave advice on how a surgeon should behave and live: not to be boastful; nor to become drunk; not to stare at women patients, especially those of high birth; and to be especially careful where you placed your hands as you treated them. He graded his fee according to the ability to pay, so the wealthy were charged the most, but having taken a large fee from the wealthy to ensure your living, he then had the means to cure the poor as an act of charity; charitable behaviour will raise a surgeon's reputation. Most importantly, the surgeon should have clean hands and finger nails. Arderne led a very adventurous life and included many interesting asides in his texts. He seems to be the first person to record that the Black Prince killed the King of Bohemia at the Battle of Crecy and took the king's ostrich feather from his helm to use as his own crest.

In Wales, the Physicians of Myddfai, had collected their own remedies, which included poisonous plants for medicinal use, including celandine, hemlock, wild lettuce, mandrake and opium poppy. The physicians had a mystical origin. During the Welsh wars for independence in the twelfth century, a widow of a farmer who had died in the fighting was left alone to raise her son. She pastured some of her cattle on the Black Mountains. One day, the son saw a beautiful lady, sitting on the shore of lake Llyn-y-Van-Vach. He fell in love, but she escaped beneath the waters and it was only after several meetings that he was able to make her his wife. She brought him great wealth, but said that she would disappear for ever if he ever struck her needlessly three times. Even a light touch was counted. For many years they lived in the village of Myddfai and together they had three sons, but inevitably the three blows were given and the lady disappeared back into the lake, taking all her animals with her. Years later the eldest son, Riwallon, unexpectedly met his mother, who told him he was destined to help cure people of disease. She gave him a bag containing medical recipes and later she taught him and his brothers the use of the local plants. The family became famed for its cures. The last physician of their descent was said to be Rice Williams MD, who died on 16 May 1842.

Paracelsus, was born about 1493/4, with the name of Philippus Aureolus Theophrastus Bombastus von Hohenheim. He was an alchemist, astrologer, doctor, and mystic. He spent much of his working life as a doctor, and believed that medicine should be practical, observing what works, and not just relying on wisdom from the past. He is credited with discovering the Doctrine of Signatures, which stated that plants carried a mark to show what they cured. The idea had been current for centuries, but Paracelsus made it more important than previously. Paracelsus was not the sort of person who trod lightly and he upset many people during his life time. He studied poisons and decided that anything could be poisonous; what was important was the dose. He wrote several books, but following his death, many writings were published under his name, although it is doubtful how many were actually his work. He died on 24 September 1541 in Salzburg. He was buried in the St Sebastian cemetery there.

William Turner, MA, 1509/10 – 13 July 1568, was born in Morpeth, Northumbria. Although from a humble family – his father was a tanner – he studied at Cambridge, gaining a BA and an MA. In 1538, he published *Libellus de re herbaria*, a catalogue of plant names, giving the names in Latin, Greek, and English. During his time at Cambridge, Turner was influenced by the Reformation Protestants Hugh Latimer and Nicholas Ridley, who were later burned by Mary in Oxford in 1555. Inspired by religious calling, Turner set out as a puritan preacher in 1540, but was arrested quite soon after. On release from prison, he went abroad, travelling across Europe to Italy where he studied and qualified in medicine. He married Jane Auder in 1542. On returning to England he became both the chaplain and the physician to the Duke of Somerset, who owned Syon House, which gave him access to some very wealthy patients. In his *The Names of Herbes,* Turner often mentions that he has not seen various plants growing in England, 'savynge in my Lordes gardine, at Syon.'

Turner was made Dean of Wells Cathedral from 1551 until 1553, when he was forced to flee once more, as the Catholic Mary came to the throne. He lived in the Rhineland, where many other English Protestants had sought refuge. In England, Mary sought to ensure the complete destruction of Turner's theological writings and he remained abroad until Elizabeth became queen. Returning to England, he lived in London, where he met Hugh Morgan, who lived to the very exceptional age of 83. Morgan was Elizabeth I's personal physician, and Turner learned much about the use of herbs from him as he prepared to write his own herbal. Turner's Herbal took a long time to prepare and write. The first volume was published in 1551, volume II, 1562 and the final part was published in 1568. Over the years, Turner had put in a lot of work to establish the correct names for plants by using his own observations. His herbal was based on earlier ones, but with his own observations and studies in England. It was the first to be published in English, not Latin as was the usual practice, setting a precedent for later authors of herbals.

Turner had returned to his old position at Wells from 1560 until 1564, when he gave up the position, spending the final four years of his life in London, where he died on 7 July 1568 at his home in Crutched Friars. He was buried in the church of St. Olave, Hart Street.

Thomas Tusser was born at Rivenhall in Essex in 1524. He became a chorister at Wallingford, near Oxford. Later, he became a member of St Paul's cathedral choir and then moved to Eton. He wrote *A Hundredth Good Pointes of Husbandrie* in 1557, which he later extended to *Five Hundred Points of Good Husbandry* in 1573. Both books are written in rhyming couplets, which make the information memorable. He married twice and had a rather chequered career that included the church, farming and trading in agriculture.

Charles de l'Écluse, sometimes referred to as Carolus Clusius, was born at Arras, on 19 February 1526. He was a doctor, botanist and gardener. He had studied medicine at Montpellier, and although he never practiced as a doctor, he probably made good use of his studies with medicinal plants because was later in charge of the Imperial Medical Garden in Vienna, and then, on becoming a professor at the University of Leiden in 1593, he helped to create one of the first botanical gardens of Europe, the Hortus Academicus. Clusius translated many books and made a study of the native alpine plants of Austria, several of which have been named after him. He died on 4 April 1609 at Leiden.

John Gerard was born in Nantwich, Cheshire, in 1545. In 1562, he became apprenticed to Alexander Mason, a barber-surgeon of the Barber-Surgeon's Company of London. Gerard completed his apprenticeship after seven years and was then admitted to the freedom of the company as a Freeman, on 9 December 1569, which allowed him to practice on his own. He seems to have been a bit of a chancer, the proverbial loveable rogue. He mentions travelling through Russia and Scandinavia in his herbal, but when he wrote to Lord Burghley in 1588, to try to gain a position at Cambridge University planting the gardens, he gave the impression that he was more widely travelled that was probably the case.

On 21 February 1578, Gerard was before the Barber Surgeons Company court accused by another freeman, Richard James, of defamation of character. James claimed that Gerard had said that James' wife had the French Pox. Gerard's response was that he would justify his claim. The case was dismissed and sent to common law. In 1595, Gerard was made a member of the Court of Assistance, which ran the Barber Surgeons. He was living in Holborn, where he had made a garden of herbs and exotic plants. He knew many prominent people who gave him plants and seeds for his garden. Gerard published a catalogue of the plants that he was growing in 1596, simply a list of the 1039 plants in the garden. In 1597, Gerard was one of several men who tried to find land to create a garden for the Society to train apprentices to recognise the plants but nothing came of the plan. It is his *Herbal* that Gerard is mostly famous for and behind it lies a dubious story of intrigue. Gerard was asked by the Queen's printer, John Norton, to translate a herbal from Latin, *Stirpium historiae pemptades sex*, that had been published by Dodoens in 1538. Henry Lytte had already made an English translation of Dodoens' earlier version of the book, *Cruydeboeck*, from Flemish, which he published as the *Niewe Herball* in 1578. It is often known as *Lyte's Herbal*. Gerard's luck was in at the time, because Norton's first choice was Dr Robert Priest, but he had died.

Gerard wrote that Priest had died before starting the project and that his work was lost, but it is suspected that Gerard obtained his papers which he edited and added to by including his own observations and stories. He included more unpublished work by his friends, Clusius and L'Obel. Gerard claimed that the herbal was the fruits of his own labours. The herbal included woodcuts that had been used in earlier herbals, but this was a fairly common practice because they were so expensive to produce. However, Gerard misidentified some of the woodcuts, although the accuracy of some of them would make it difficult to know what they were intended to be. *The Great Herball*, also known as the *General Historie of Plantes* was published in 1597.

Some would say that Gerard was a plagiarist, but in today's sense that does not really apply as all the people he was said to have copied were all copying Dioscorides. That he did not credit the work of others is another matter and probably true. Gerard made many errors, but it is the stories that he tells and his own comments that make the book such a good read. Barnacle Geese growing on trees; notes of where he has seen the plants growing with his own eyes, and of wives falling on their husband's fists; they all add a quirky view on contemporary life. Personally, I forgive him his wrongs doings; later herbals became rather dry reading, even if more scientifically accurate. The 1633 and 1636 editions of the book contained additional plants and were corrected by an apothecary, Thomas

Johnson, who included his own notes on Gerard's original writings. It is reproductions of Johnson's editions that can be bought today. Gerard died in February 1612 and was buried at the church of St. Andrew, Holborn. The site of his grave has been lost.

John Parkinson was born in 1567, so he was a contemporary of Gerard. He was a trained apothecary, being James I's personal apothecary and a founder member of the Worshipful Society of Apothecaries, which was set up in 1617. He wrote two major works on plants and gardens, both published before the unrest that would be caused by the Civil War.

Parkinson had a garden at Long Acre in Covent Garden, where he grew his plants, including new introductions to the country as he was friends with John Tradescant the Elder, as well as many prominent herbalists and gardeners including Gerard and Matthias de l'Obel, who was supervisor of Edward de la Zouche's gardens at Highgate. Parkinson's book, *Paradisi in Sole Paradisus Terrestris,* was published in 1629. The title is a scholarly pun. Paradisi refers to a park-like garden, in Sole means in the sun, so a pun on Parkinson. In full it means, *Parkinson's Terrestrial Paradise*. He dedicated the book to Queen Henrietta Maria, the wife of Charles I. The book's title page has a woodcut showing the garden of Eden, suggesting that we could aspire to creating our own Eden on earth. The first chapters describe the selection of the ideal site and how to deal with the problems faced by the would-be gardener. Next, there is the laying out of the pleasure garden and some suggested patterns for knot gardens. He continues to the outlandish plants, by which he means, foreign plants, then the English flowers which he follows with notes on cultivation. The section titled, *The Garden of Pleasant Flowers*, begins with the suitably regal flower, the Crown Imperial. This section takes up the greater part of the book and includes descriptions of each plant and accurately rendered woodcut illustrations of some of the plants. The second part deals with the kitchen garden and includes herbs and their uses, the third part deals with the orchard and fruit trees, after which there is a corollary of non-fruiting trees that are useful in gardens, including the medicinal use of poisonous plants that are suitable to grow in gardens.

Parkinson's other book was *Theatrum Botanicum, The Botanical Theatre* or *Theatre of Plants,* published in 1640, when Parkinson was 73. The dedication this time was to the king himself, Charles I, who gave Parkinson the title of *Botanicus Regis Primarius*, or Royal Botanist of the First Rank; it may have been an honour, but it was an unpaid one. Theatrum Botanicum was a very ambitious herbal, written to correct past mistakes and include all the new plants from Virginia and the middle east. Parkinson wrote a description of each plant, gave its medical uses and a provided a woodcut illustration. Unlike Gerard, he openly acknowledged the work of l'Obel, Dr Bonham and others at the front of the book. Parkinson died in 1650, and was buried on 6 August at St Martin-in-the-Fields, London. His work continued to be consulted by gardeners and apothecaries for years afterwards.

Nicholas Culpepper is one of the most famous authors of an herbal and he certainly did lead an adventurous life. Things did not begin well for Nicholas. He was born on 18 October 1616 and never knew his father as he had died thirteen days before he was born. His father, a clergyman, had only recently inherited the manor of Ockley, in Surrey, but on his death the manor was taken out of the family. Nicholas was brought up at his mother's family home at Isfield, Sussex. His grandfather, the Reverend William Attersole, was a strict puritan, with little regard for the King. He taught the boy Latin and Greek which Nicholas put to good use by reading books on astrology, herbs and medicine in William's well-stocked library. Aged sixteen, Nicholas was sent to Cambridge to study theology in order to become a priest, but he spent as much time as possible studying medicine. He became a typical student, spending a lot of his time in the taverns, smoking and playing bowls and tennis. It is not surprising that he failed to complete his course. Before leaving for Cambridge Nicholas had fallen in love with Judith Rivers, a local heiress. As they both knew that her family would not approve the match, they planned to elope, marry and go to the Netherlands until the families came to terms with their marriage. They agreed to meet near Lewes. Tragedy struck when Judith's coach was struck by lightning and she died. Nicholas was devastated and fell into a depression. His mother died not long after.

It was William Attersole who had the idea that his ward could become an apothecary and maintain his interest in medicine. He was made an apprentice to the apothecary, Francis Drake, who had a shop in Threadneedle Street, Bishopsgate. Culpepper had to learn to identify the herbs he would need and was taught by none other than Thomas Johnson who had recently edited the later version of Gerard's herbal. Whilst in London, Culpepper became friends with William Lilly, the astrologer, who taught him how the stars influenced disease. Culpepper would later incorporate astrology into his work and publications. In 1640, Culpepper, now twenty-four, married Alice Field, aged fifteen. She had inherited a large amount of money, which Culpepper used to build a new house in

Red Lion Street, next door to the inn of the same name. Here he treated the poor for nothing most of the time and his reputation spread. He was outspoken on the high charges of the apothecaries and physicians; he also objected to some of their practices, disapproving of blood-letting and purging in particular. When the Civil War began, he enlisted for Parliament in 1642 and fought at Edgehill. In 1643, he was made a captain of infantry, and he raised a group of sixty men to fight at the siege of Gloucester He was badly injured in the shoulder by a musket ball on the journey home when the road was blocked outside Newbury. Once King Charles was executed, the strict laws on publishing were removed and Culpepper took advantage of the new freedoms to publish a book on medicine in plain English that everybody could read without the need for a long schooling in Latin. His book, The English Physitian, was his own translation of the London Pharmacopoeia of the apothecaries, with his own emphasis on the importance of astrology and the Doctrine of Signatures. The plants that Culpepper chose for his medicines were either commonly growing in most gardens or could be collected from the local countryside. His purpose was to allow the poor to treat themselves safely and cheaply and avoid the large fees charged by the doctors.

Culpepper died 10 January 1654, aged 38, soon after completing the book for which he is still famous. He had been ill for some time, still suffering from the wound he had received eleven years before; years of working long hours as a physician and writing his books finally wore him out. He remained a radical until the day he died and never succumbed to the easy life that could have been his.

William Coles, 1626-1662, was a contemporary of Culpepper, and like him, he studied the use of English plants for his book, The Art of Simpling. An introduction to the Knowledge and Gathering of Plants in 1656. Simples are herbal remedies made of only one plant. Many herbal remedies included several plants to treat a disease. Coles used the Doctrine of Signatures to help him to decide on the use of each herb, saying;

> '...yet the mercy of God... maketh... herbs for the use of Men, and not only stamped upon them (as upon every Man) a distinct form, but also given them particular Signatures, whereby a man may read, even in legible Characters, the use of them.'

But Coles admits that not all plants do have a signature. His answer is that god left mankind a few things to discover for himself, and:

> 'As in stinking weeds and poisonous plants, how that they were not created in vain, but have their uses. They would not be without their

use, if they were good for nothing else but to exercise the Industry of Man to weed them out.'

Coles was very much an establishment man and could not resist making an attack on Culpepper, who was well-known for his anti-establishment sentiments. Having noted the lack of plant knowledge of most of his fellow countrymen, Coles wrote;

'I go not about to deceive them with a few empty notions, as Mr. Culpepper hath done, telling them many nonsensical stores of I know not what; when it is evident to those that knew him, or are able to judge of his writings, that he understood not those plant he trod upon.'

In 1657, Coles printed *Adam in Eden, or Nature's Paradise*. The book is a much-expanded form of the first, dealing with the plants individually and in much more detail. Perhaps he was competing for a part of Culpepper's readership.

John Pechey, or Peachey, 1655-1716, received a BA and an MA at Oxford. On 22 December 1684, he was granted a licentiate of the College of Physicians in London. He lived and worked at the Angel and Crown, Basing Lane, in the City of London. He was called before the College of Physicians in November 1688 for the way he practiced, as he was acting not so much as a physician, but as an apothecary. He was reprimanded, and having not changed his ways, he was fined £4, which he did not pay, and was later fined £8. The matter was finally resolved in 1689. He wrote several books, but *The Compleat Herbal of Physical Plants*, published in 1694, and reprinted in 1707 was the book the gave the use of different plants.

Richard Brook was another idealist who wanted to carry on from where Culpepper had left off. He was a botanist and a founder member of the *Huddersfield Naturalists' Society*; the first recorded meeting being held at his house on 21 July 1850. The Society's members were all working men. Brook had been a tailor, a cotton spinner, a shop keeper and later became a printer and book seller. He had been an active Chartist and used his publications to air his political views. He often advertised 'Dr Torrens Pills' and it is very likely that he was the said Dr Torrens. In 1847, he began to publish part of *Culpepper's Herbal Improved: A New Family Herbal, or a History & Description of all the British and Foreign Plants, which are useful to man, either as food, medicine, farming purposes, or in the arts and manufactures.* Various editions of this continued to be printed until the 1880s and later authors, including Mrs Maud Grieve, often referred to his work. Brook was not one to miss a chance for self-publicity. One edition of the book, contains the following:

'At a Meeting of the Liverpool Pharmaceutical Society, Doctor Birbeck Nevens, in speaking of the use of herbs in medicines, took the opportunity to speak highly of Culpepper's Herbal, improved by Brook, "AS BEING FREE OF HUMBUG, and valuable in those cases in which the author of it spoke from personal experience."- PHARMACEUTICAL JOURNAL, May 1867.'

Following after this note, Brook mentioned that he was writing an even larger and more thorough book, which would be available shortly.

Brook wrote with the same purpose as Culpepper, to provide a cheap guide to self-medication for the poor. He read widely and edited his book to make it easy to read and included practical growing information of the plants, how to make medicines and warnings when plants were too dangerous to use without proper training.

The last of the old-style herbals was written by Mrs Maud Grieve. She was born Sophie Emma Magdalene Law on 4 May 1858, in Islington, London. Her father died in 1864, after which she moved to Beckenham where she was brought up by relatives. She received an inheritance of £1,000 when her uncle died. It is not known what she did next, but she later visited India where she met and married a Scotsman, William Grieve, in 1883. Grieve managed a paper mill near Calcutta until 1894, when the couple returned to England. They eventually settled at Chalfont Common, just north of Chalfont St Peter. William designed the house, Maud designed the garden. During the First World War Maud concentrated on growing herbs for the war effort because most medicinal herbs by that time had been imported and supplies were running low; many were the basis for painkillers. Maud helped to set up the National Herb Growing Association which was mostly run by women of the Women's Farm and Garden Union with the backing of the Pharmaceutical Society. The association was in existence from 1914 to 1917. She later became the President of the British Guild of Herb Growers, founded in 1918. She continued to be involved with herbs for the rest of her life and wrote monographs on individual herbs. These were edited and compiled by Hilda Leyel and published in 1931 under the title of *A Modern Herbal*.

Maud died on 21 December 1941, but her legacy lives on, as her influential book continues to be studied because it includes traditional uses and the current uses and medical information such as the dosage, and detailed cultivation notes for commercial production.

THE DANGERS OF THE POTTING SHED

It is hard in our modern world of strict controls on chemicals, to realise that things have been much laxer in the past. A whole arsenal of lethal poisons was lurking in the potting shed of the walled garden, or in the garden or allotment shed.

Most early gardening books tell you as much about killing things as growing them. In the days before supermarkets, growing your own food was a matter of survival. A Head Gardener's job was at risk if he could not provide a constant supply of food throughout the year and as the Potato Famine of the 1840s proved, when things went wrong the results could be devastating.

The syringes and sprayers used to spray plants with chemicals carried the nickname of Widow Makers. The fine droplets of deadly poisons were sprayed up into fruit trees, allowing them to waft in the air and be breathed into the lungs of the gardeners, or soak into their clothing and boots and thence onto the skin. Protection often amounted to little more than a wide brimmed hat and an apron. The prolonged use of these sprays could result in an early death.

It is hardly surprising that Agatha Christie's murderers often chose poison. They lurked in the kitchen, the medicine cupboard and the shed at the bottom of the garden because poisons were commonly in daily use. Arsenic was the toxic ingredient of fly papers; strychnine and cyanide were kept for killing vermin. The novels reflected real life.

Cyanide occurs naturally. Some algae, bacteria and fungi produce forms of it, but it is mostly found in the kernels of bitter almonds, cherries and peaches and also in apple pips. A cider maker from Norfolk once told me that the reason why west country cider drinkers were reputed to go doolally and the Norfolk ones were not, was down to the different ways in which the cider apples were prepared. In Norfolk the apples were pulped, whereas in the West country they were crushed between mill stones, which also crushed the pips, releasing very small amounts of cyanide into the juice. In the past, part of an agricultural worker's wages was a gallon of ale or cider, and most of them were working six days a week at least, so they were taking in a lot of cyanide laced cider that gradually sent them slightly mad. How true that is I have no idea, but it is an intriguing story.

Hydrogen Cyanide is a more recent poison. It was discovered by a Swedish chemist Carl Wilhelm Scheele, in 1782. He prepared it from the chemical dye, Prussian Blue, first made in about 1704, which lead to its common English name of Prussic Acid. Cyanide was used to destroy wasp nests, pests and people and rather surprisingly, it was also loaded into the harpoons used to kill whales. Hydrogen cyanide gas pellets have been used to gas moles and rabbits. The pellets are delivered into the holes from a long plastic sealed tube, looking rather like a light sabre used in the *Star Wars* films. The holes are sealed and the pellets react with soil moisture to release the poisonous gas. As the pellets can also react to atmospheric moisture the product has to be used with great care and the operatives have to be properly trained, licenced and work in pairs. This is the gas used by the Nazis in their extermination camps and by the American states that executed their criminals in gas chambers from 1924-2010.

Fly papers were common in many households. Packets of fly papers were obtainable from a chemist. An individual paper would be placed in a dish of water to which a small amount of sugar or some other substance, such as honey, to attract the flies, had been added. When the flies drank the sweetened water, they died. It could literally be a honey trap. The papers were often prepared by the local chemist and to prevent accidental misuse, the fly papers also contained quassia to make it bitter to the taste and a brown dye was often added to make the liquid visually unattractive. There are numerous cases of women soaking the fly papers to extract the arsenic to murder an unwanted husband.

Two Irish women, Margaret Higgins and her elder sister, Catherine Flannagan who were living in Liverpool during the early 1880s, took advantage of the easy access to arsenic fly papers to profitably murder people whom they had previously insured through burial funds. After several successful claims, they were apprehended and tried. Both women were hanged on 3 March 1884. Such was the interest in the story that Madame Tussauds included models of the women in their Chamber of Horrors.

During the 1960s and early 1970s, Paraquat was a popular non-selective weed killer for clearing top growth in decorative areas and paving. Anybody could obtain it very easily. Unfortunately, if ingested at full strength there is no antidote. It can be up to thirty days before the patient finally dies. In the past, before the chemical became more strictly controlled, the usual problem was a result of a gardener making a mix, spraying the weeds, but then having some left over, putting it an old soft drinks bottle. The chemical looked very similar to a cola drink and although the liquid causes burning sensations in the throat, if quickly swigged some of the fluid could easily be ingested. Several children have died from Paraquat poisoning. I met a nurse who had treated children who had drunk Paraquat mixtures; she told me that there was nothing that they could do, but to try to lessen their pain as much as possible as they waited for the inevitable.

There has only been one case of murder using Paraquat in the UK, when Susan Barber poisoned the gravy that she made for her husband's pie in 1981; she was found guilty of murder in 1982. Elsewhere in the world, there have been numerous murders using Paraquat, including a case in Japan during 1985, when possibly twelve people were killed by Paraquat poisoned drinks that were left in, or close to, drinks vending machines. Vending machines of all types were very popular in Japan and were rarely vandalised or tampered with. The drinks were bottled and sometimes a poisoned drink was left in the machine so that the victim thought that they had obtained a free drink, and were less wary than they may otherwise have been. The first murder took place in Fukuyama, Hiroshima on 30 April. More murders took place between 11 September and 17 November. The police were unable to find any evidence to catch the murderer, but the murders ceased as quickly as they began when the drinks machine owners posted warnings not to drink any drinks that may be left in the machine or close by.

Paraquat was a popular method of suicide among Welsh hill farmers with ailing farms. If you could get a mouthful down the chances of surviving were minimal unless treated very quickly. As a method of suicide Paraquat is still popular in many parts of the world because it is cheap and readily available. Apparently, the United States drug enforcers still use Paraquat to spray illegally grown cannabis plants.

To maintain a perfect weed-free lawn would once have required a large labour force, which could be put to work manually digging out the buttercups, clover, daisies, dandelions and other weeds that spoiled the perfection of the finely manicured lawn. The first chemical weed killers included arsenious acid, hydrochloric acid, sulphuric acid, copper sulphate, white arsenic and Prussian blue. For use on the lawns, the weeds could be painted with the chemicals or the chemicals could be injected into weeds with special syringe-like equipment. Equally dangerous chemicals, such as hydrochloric acid and mercuric acid were used to kill worms.

If the chemicals needed to maintain the lawn were dangerous, those used on the golf course were equally potent. Conor Burke, an Irish doctor, treated a man with an inexplicable case of non-viral hepatitis. The cause was later given as being due to the golfer's habit of licking his ball clean at each hole before teeing off. The golf course regularly used selective weed killers to control weeds in the turf; as the balls ran across the grass they picked up residue which the golfer then ingested as he licked the balls. The long-term effects resulted in liver damage, which in turn lead to hepatitis.

Brian Mayo was another golfer who suffered the effects of weed killer on his golf balls; he used to lick his ball before taking a putt. In 1980, this lead to him being in a coma for eleven days and losing both of his legs after contracting meningitis. In 1982, another golfer, Navy Lieutenant George M. Prior, played thirty-six holes at the Army-Navy Country Club, Arklington, Virginia. Towards the end of the game he was complaining of a headache. During the evening, he developed a rash and had symptoms of fever and nausea. After four days, he was taken to hospital and died ten days later when his major organs failed and eighty per cent of his skin was blistered and burned. The cause was attributed to his custom of carrying his golf tees in his mouth, resulting in him ingesting a dangerous amount of Daconil, an approved fungicide, that was sprayed onto the grass at the course twice a week. Unfortunately, Prior was particularly sensitive to the chemical, which led to his unexpected allergic reaction.

I have met people who think that only natural products should be used in the garden. Mineral pesticides are natural, in the strictest sense of the word, but if they really intend to mean plant based pesticides, then some of those have now been banned too. One of the most popular was Derris, used as a contact insecticide since the mid nineteenth century. It is produced from the root of Derris elliptica, native to Asia, a climbing plant that has leaves and flowers similar to wisteria. The crushed root has also been used to stun fish by throwing it into the water. The active ingredient extracted from the tree root is Rotenone, which has been linked to the progressive brain disorder Parkinson's Disease. The dust could also affect breathing. A retired pharmacist told me of her experience of Derris;

> 'When I was a student at Chelsea School of Pharmacy, I once tasted Derris root, which I recorded as tasteless. Minutes later my mouth became paralysed and numb which was very unpleasant. I suppose this would count as accidental, but self-inflicted, poisoning.'

Derris Dust is now banned in Britain as an insecticide, as is DDT, which was as equally popular in the 1960s and was used to kill myriad pests, including caterpillars and insects, but it spread throughout the food chain, poisoning the birds that ate the insects and eventually killing birds of prey. It was equally lethal to humans in the long-term, especially when used by untrained gardeners who ignored the mixing instructions and never wore protective clothing as most books only recommended old clothing when you were spraying. It was banned in 1972.

Another plant based insecticide is Pyrethrum, extracted from *Chrysanthemum cinerariifolium*. The flower has been used by the Chinese as an insecticide since about 1000 BC. The flowers can be dried and powdered, then sprinkled over the plants you want to protect from insects. Pyrethrins are now made synthetically.

Every year more chemicals are banned as research shows that they are not as safe as was once thought. Aldrin was used to kill insects in the soil. Lindane was used as an insecticide, but also to treat head lice. Sodium chlorate was mostly used to control weeds in paving, but before it was banned, a man I knew used it on his flower beds. He used more chemical than the instructions directed – and nothing would grow there for several years. Council gardeners used to scatter *Dichlobenil* granules, over shrub beds and on hard surfaces to stop weeds growing, but it remained active in the soil and was moved by rainwater, so it is now banned, along with other residual herbicides. Nowadays, professional gardeners who use any chemical spray at work have to be trained and hold licences, but despite this, it is still fairly common to see brown foot prints on the grass where the person spraying weeds has walked the chemical across the turf. The armoury that gardeners used to kill pests, fungal infections and weeds has been getting smaller over the years; and we and the environment are probably healthier for it.

Early gardening books were often as much about killing things as growing plants, because if the food plants did not grow, you would go hungry. For many householders in the western world, this is no longer a major concern; we can go to the supermarket. It is worth bearing in mind, though, that, even today, many accidents still occur in the garden.

A CONUNDRUM

As was common during the Regency period, Jane Austen would pass the time with games. At the Jane Austen House Museum at Chawton in Hampshire, there is one of Jane's conundrums hanging in a frame on a wall. I saw this many years ago and now include it in my talk and I have decided to include it here. I confess that I could not guess the answer and after years of giving the talk, it was ten years before somebody gave the correct answer without any help.

The only clue that I shall give is that the answer is one of the plants in this book:

'When my first is a task to a young girl of Spirit,

And my second confines her to finish the piece.

How hard is her fate, but how hard is her merit,

If by taking my whole she effects her release.'

AQUILEGIA

Aquilegia is said to have been named from the Latin word for an eagle, because the long spikes of the flowers resemble an eagle's talons. The common name of columbine derives from Latin for a dove, as, if you hold the flower upright, so that the spikes are pointing into the air, the flower now resembles a circle of sitting doves; rather similar to the doves that used to sit around a fountain in a medieval garden. The Culverwort name for aquilegia name derives from doves, a culver house being another name for a dovecote.

Genus: *Aquilegia*
Species: *vulgaris*
Family: Ranunculaceae
Other Names:
  Columbine.
  Granny's Bonnet.
  Culver wort.
  Herba Leonis.
Herbaceous Perennial
Active Constituents:
Cardiogenic toxins.

Aquilegia grows to 90cm tall and has divided, glaucous leaves that remain attractive even when the flowers have finished. The stems and the leaves are said to be safe to eat, but the seeds and roots are poisonous, although various experts seem to disagree. In Britain, neither the Horticultural Trades Association nor The Royal Horticultural Society include it in their list of potentially harmful plants; but the University of California does list it as a harmful plant. Let the buyer beware.

The flowers of the European species tend to range in colour from white to pink, and from blue to violet; sometimes in multi-petalled forms. Aquilegia prefers damp woodland shade and if it is grown in situations that become too hot where the soil dries out, the leaves may be affected by mildew. The best cure is to cut off all the leaves, dig in some organic matter and to water when the weather becomes dry.

Many early writers ignored aquilegia as a medicinal plant. Gerard said that there was no practical use for the plant, other than for their beauty in gardens, houses and garlands and Thomas Tusser agreed with him, as he included aquilegia in his list of plants for windows and pots.

Aquilegia was meant to be good for quinsy and swellings of the throat, or as a cure for a sore mouth or sore throat. Both Parkinson and Culpepper related that in Spain it was known that some people ate the root at breakfast for several days if they were troubled by kidney stones. Parkinson also mentioned that the leaves and root could be added to Ambergris and wine for those affected by the swoonings. The seed could be powdered and used as a medicine for jaundice and other liver problems for which it was still being recommended in the early nineteenth century.

Clusius, the Flemish botanist, wrote that one of the most important physicians of Bruges, Franciscus Rapard, often powdered the seed and made a drink of it to help women to have a speedy delivery of a child in the case of difficult births. He advised a second draught if the first was not working effectively.

A more unusual use was that a blue syrup was made using the flowers to test for the acidity or alkalinity of substances, which was said to be better than using syrup of violets.

The plant is high in vitamin C, and has rather dubiously been used for scurvy; but due to its poisonous nature, nowadays it has gone back to being grown for the other main use that was mentioned in the past; as a pretty flower to decorate our gardens.

ASARABACA

Asarum is said by some authorities to be a native plant to Britain, although I have yet to see it growing wild. Turner said that he only knew of it growing in gardens, so it may have escaped into the wild. It is a low growing plant with shiny leathery leaves that are no more than 15cm above the ground. The purplish flowers hide beneath them, so if you wish to see them closely it is better to grow the plant in a pot rather than get down on your knees to admire the flowers; not that they are particularly spectacular. The seeds have an extra part on them called, an elaiosome,

Genus: *Asarum*
Species: *europaeum*
Family: Aristolochiaceae
Other Names:
    Wild Ginger.
    Asara bacca.
    Fole Foot.
    Asaron.
Hardy Perennial
Active Constituents:
    Asaron.
    Methyleugenol.
    Bornyl- acetate.

which in this case looks like a small caterpillar but is also tasty to the ants, who for a small gift of food, help to distribute the seeds.

Asarabaca is one of the purging plants and the herbals suggest that it is better administered in incremental doses to avoid over-dosing the patient. This is one of the plants that would be better administered as an enema.

Dioscorides says that the root had a smell that was rather like cinnamon, most other writers say it is more like ginger, hence the common name. Having tasted the root, I would say it was more like ginger. Dioscorides mentioned that Asarum was good to encourage the menses, so it was probably used to induce abortions in larger doses, and was still being used much later because John Pechey said that, wenches use 'the decoction of it too frequently, when they think they are with child'. Most authors agreed that the plant induced upward and downward purging.

Brook said that the powdered root was a powerful snuff for clearing the head of headaches, dizziness, drowsiness and head cold. It would also clear the loss of hearing caused by blocked sinuses. Four or five grains snuffed at night would be enough to cause a discharge of matter from the nose by the following morning, which could even continue throughout the day. The warning was given that this should not be a frequent habit as it could be dangerous.

AUTUMN CROCUS

The Autumn Crocus is not actually a crocus at all, being in a different family. Colchicums are often called naked ladies because they flower alone in the autumn without the leaves. The flowers are 15cm tall and are usually a pale lilac colour, but they can be darker or even white, such as *Colchicum autumnale* 'Alboplenum'. There are other garden cultivars that are very attractive, including, 'Waterlily', which is a multi-petal form.

Genus: *Colchicum*
Species: *autumnale*
Family: Colchicaceae
Other Names:
Autumn Crocus.
Meadow Saffron.
Naked Ladies.
Corm
Active Constituents:
Colchinine.

The broad leaves are about 30 cm long and appear early in the spring and could easily be mistaken for Wild Garlic by somebody who simply looked at the leaves without checking for a garlic odour; but this is unlikely to be frequent occurrence as *Colchicum* is no longer very common in the wild in Britain. But the mistake has been made and there are several documented cases. The symptoms of poisoning are said to be similar to those of arsenic poisoning and also of cholera.

Dioscorides said that the if you ate the bulbs you would die by choking, much the same as from eating poisonous mushrooms. He said that he mentions this because he did not want anybody to eat colchicum by mistake. If by chance you did, by drinking cow's milk, then the same remedies as used for mushroom poisoning *may* help. In Scotland during 2003, a 76-year-old man ate two Colchicum plants, mistakenly thinking that they were Wild Garlic, which he had heard would be good for the liver damage that he had sustained through alcohol misuse. After two hours, he began to feel nauseous. Within four to five he was vomiting and suffered from watery diarrhoea. After twelve hours, he was taken to the Emergency Department of the local hospital and placed in Intensive Care. For the first day of hospitalisation, his only symptoms were of a gastro-intestinal nature. On the second day, his breathing began to fail and he was placed on a ventilator, whilst his heart rate fell drastically. On the third day, he began to bleed from the nose, and later in the day he died of heart failure despite attempts at resuscitation. It was estimated that he had only eaten 5g. of the leaves. There is a chance he may have survived if his liver had been working properly.

Another case recorded in 2004 involved a 71-year-old woman who again mistook the plant for Wild Garlic. She arrived at hospital twelve hours after eating the colchicum with the usual symptoms. She developed alopecia after three weeks, and had many gastro-intestinal problems, but she survived and after five months there were no signs that she had poisoned herself.

There are recorded cases of suicide attempts by ingesting colchicums. In 1967, a sixteen-year-old girl, who had threatened suicide on several occasions, ate over sixteen flowers of *Colchicum autumnale*. She was admitted to hospital the following morning, but only survived for another day. In 2001 a case was recorded of what appears to have been a suicide attempt, when a man ate forty colchicum flowers, but this time he survived. In August 2011, a man in the southern region of Karnataka State in South India ate *Gowri Gedde*, the local name for *Colchicum autumnale* and died three days later. But suicide using this method has a long history.

During the early 1830s there had been a drastic rise in suicide in Paris and Monsieur Dupin carried out research, before reaching his conclusion, in which he attributed the rise to the 'recurring political excitement' of the previous six years'. The number of suicides had risen from 269 in 1830, to 477 in 1835, with the majority of the suicides aged between 31 and 50 years of age, and many had chosen Colchicine as the method of death. In comparison, the London records showed that between 1834 and 1835 there had only been 83 cases of suicide. Thankfully, the British did not take to committing suicide during the turmoil of attempting to leave the European Union!

In the early nineteenth century, colchicum was being used once more as a cure for gout under the name of *Tinctura Colchici*, which probably made it more widely available. Contrary to what has often been reported, colchicine, the poison in the plant, has been used to commit murder. Catherine Wilson was born in 1842, and lived in Boston, Lincolnshire where she worked as a nurse. She began living with a man named James Dixon, who later died and although not deemed suspicious at the time, it was later thought that he had been poisoned by Wilson because she was tired of him drinking too much. A bottle containing colchicine was found in the room, which Wilson said she was using to treat his rheumatic fever. An autopsy had been recommended by the doctor, but Mrs. Wilson persuaded him against it, saying that James Dixon had a fear of being cut up after death. In 1862, Wilson began work for Mrs Sarah Carnell as a live-in nurse. Mrs Carnell was impressed with her nurse and altered her will, favouring Wilson. Sometime after, Wilson gave Mrs. Carnell a drink, saying that it would warm her. Carnell took a sip and spat it out because it had burned her mouth, later noticing that it had burned the bed sheets. Wilson fled to London, but was arrested and charged with attempted murder in April 1862. The drink had been found to contain enough sulphuric acid to kill fifty people. Wilson claimed that the pharmacist had made a mistake in mixing the medicine. As this could not be proven one way or the other she was acquitted, although the point was raised that if this had really been the case the bottle would have split or become too hot to handle before she could get home. Her sense of relief of the trial's outcome was short-lived because she was immediately re-arrested. Some of Wilson's previous patients, all of whom had died after altering their wills, were exhumed by the police and traces of poison were found in their bodies. She was charged with the murder of seven people but was only tried for the murder of one, Mrs Maria Soames, who had died in 1856. It was alleged that the various patients had all received treatment for gout, for which one of the common remedies was colchicine. During the trial, Mrs. Soames daughter mentioned that on numerous occasions, Wilson had given her mother a drink of brandy and eggs, that she was told would be good for her. However, her mother was usually sick soon after taking the drink, which had always been prepared elsewhere by Wilson.

The renowned toxicologist, Alfred Swaine Taylor, who in 1848 had published a book, *On Poisons in Relation to Medical Jurisprudence and Medicine,* was called as an expert witness. He gave evidence that helped to discern whether the cause of death was possibly cholera or poisoning. Tests for the common poisons such as arsenic, antimony and mercury had proved negative. Taylor said that he had not known of colchicum being used as a poison during the last fifteen years, but in this case, he believed it had been, and that poisoning, and not a disease that had caused the death. Dr Thomas Nunnelly was called to verify Taylor's conclusions, and he agreed on all the points discussed, the case for the prosecution, although the defence pleaded that after such a long time the evidence of poisoning was not reliable. This time, the jury was persuaded and Wilson was sentenced to death by hanging. She firmly denied being guilty, before she was led out for execution. She was publicly hanged at Newgate Gaol on at 8 am Monday 20 October 1862, in front of a crowd of 20,000 onlookers, the last woman to be publicly hanged in London. Although she had been tried and found guilty of the one murder, it was generally accepted that there had probably been many more. A broadside ballad was written, as was the usual case in such circumstances, to the tune of *Ave Maria*, with the chorus of:

'Catherine Wilson thus died she
A dreadful death upon the gallows high.'

A waxwork of her was displayed at Madame Tussauds.

BASIL

Basil? That is not poisonous, is it? Well, thankfully, no; but it does have a death associated with it through the story of *Isabella and the Pot of Basil*. The story was told by Boccaccio in *The Decameron*, where it was told on the fourth day, as the fifth tale, but he names the girl as Lisabetta. Keats later told the story in sixty-three verses of poetry, changing the girl's name to Isabella. The story was popular with the Pre-Raphaelite artists who based many of their paintings on medieval stories. I shall now recount the tale in my own way.

Genus: *Ocimum*
Species: *basilicum*
Family: Lamiaceae
Other Names:
   Basil.
Tender Annual
Active Constituents:
   Eugenol.

Isabella was a young girl who lived in Messina. She had three brothers who had inherited a thriving business from their father who had recently died. The brothers spent all of their time tending to the business and trading in their shop. Isabella became very lonely, and very bored. The business began to prosper, so much so that the brothers soon realised that they needed some extra help, and so they employed a local young man named Lorenzo to assist them. Isabella and Lorenzo quickly became friends, perhaps a little too friendly the brothers thought; and even more so when one of the brothers noticed Isabella quietly entering Lorenzo's room one night...

The brothers were unsure what to do. Isabella was of a marriageable age and they had already begun to wonder who would be a suitable match for her; somebody with a position and wealth, of that they were sure. One thing they were certain of, Lorenzo was of too lowly a status to be a suitable suitor for their sister. More importantly though, they were also worried that their sister's honour and reputation was at stake. And so, they devised a plan.

One day the brothers told Isabella that they were off to a nearby city to visit the fair and carry out some trade. They were taking Lorenzo with them and would return in a few days' time. They rode off and a few days later they returned, with tales of how much money they had made at the fair.

'But where's Lorenzo?' Isabella asked.

'Oh! Trade was very good, so we sent him on to another city to carry out more business for us. He will return soon enough.'

But he did not.

'Where is Lorenzo?' Isabella kept asking. 'Why hasn't he returned yet?'

'Business must be better than we expected. He must still be working' the brothers told her.

Yet still Lorenzo never returned, and still Isabella kept asking, 'Where is Lorenzo? When will he come home?'

'We don't know!' the brothers told her crossly, 'and why do you keep asking after Lorenzo. He has probably started work with somebody else. Stop worrying and forget about him!'

But Isabella could not stop worrying and neither could she forget her beloved Lorenzo. One night she had a dream; more of a nightmare. Lorenzo appeared to her. His clothes were torn and splattered with blood and soil. 'Your brothers murdered me' he said, 'and they had buried me in a shallow grave close to the edge of a wood.' He then told Isabella how to find his grave. Poor Isabella could scarcely sleep the rest of the night. In the morning she rose early, woke her maid and together they rode to the wood that Lorenzo had described. They searched the forest edge and soon discovered the grave exactly where he had told them. Isabella wept but was unsure as to what she should do next. She took out her knife and severed Lorenzo's head from the body and carefully wrapped it in her cloak.

When she arrived home the brothers were away at work. Isabella found a finely decorated flowerpot, put some soil in the bottom and gently lowered Lorenzo's head inside and then carefully filled the pot with soil. Into the soil she placed some of the best basil plants of Salerno. According to the story, the basil thrived. As well it might, as it had blood and bone fertiliser at its roots. Isabella swooned over the pot and gently watered it with her tears. The brothers wondered about Isabella's strange behaviour. One day, when she was not at home, they picked up the pot and smashed it to smithereens on the floor. Out rolled the remains of Lorenzo's head - why it had not stunk the house out by now we are not told. The brothers quickly realised that Isabella knew what they had done. They cleared up the remains, and hid them away in a secret place and fled to Naples. Isabella returned and was utterly distraught when she could not find her pot of basil, and after much wailing and weeping, she died of a broken heart.

So, the next time you eat a tomato and mozzarella salad, with basil - please remember poor Isabella…

But basil does have many other uses. Growing basil in a greenhouse as a companion plant with tomatoes helps to discourage whitefly; which I can vouch for, and some say that the tomatoes will also taste better.

The Greek Orthodox church uses basil to sprinkle holy water, so it is good for removing demons too. Basil is not completely safe, in high doses basil is said to be narcotic and the essential oil may cause a rash on sensitive skin. Although basil may not be too poisonous for people, it is being tested for potential toxicity to control mosquitos.

BAY

The Bay tree likes to grow in warm climates, Gerard wrote that he had never seen a bay tree growing in Denmark, Poland, Sweden, Russia or any other cold country that he had visited on his travels. In most of Britain it will grow well in a sheltered position with free-draining soil and it is fairly tolerant of shade. The leaves are dark green and have an aromatic odour. The small flowers are a yellowish green colour. Bay is dioecious, so the male and female flowers are carried on separate trees. The berries are black and contain a single seed. The leaves are used to flavour food; the berries are pressed to extract the oil. Bay can reach a height of 8m in Britain, but will be taller when grown in good conditions.

Genus: *Laurus*
Species: *nobilis*
Family: Lauraceae
Other Names:
  Bay Tree.
  Bay Laurel.
  Laurel.
  Sweet Bay.
  Roman Laurel.
Evergreen Tree/Shrub
Active Constituents:
  Cineol. Eugenol.
  Geraniol. Linalool.
  Terpineol.

When it is planted in gardens, the bay tree is rarely allowed to grow naturally because it is traditionally grown as topiary, often being shaped like a lollipop on a single stem, or sometimes with three stems plaited together. In areas where hard frost is likely, many people move their bare-stemmed bay topiary to somewhere sheltered. I have seen people used polystyrene water-pipe insulation tubes that they have fitted over the bare trunks to protect them. If the trunk is affected by the cold, the bark splits, cutting off the sap supply to the branches, which then die; but the plant will often sprout again from the roots. If you have an established plant with strong roots you can be quite brutal with pruning. I once cut down an old bay tree that had quite a single, thick trunk. It regrew from the roots, throwing up dozens of single shoots that all eventually grew to the height of the original tree; so I had to cut them all down again. I have grown bay as a tree or a tall shrub in cold areas and the worse that often happens is that a few leaves may be burned by frost. The trunks being protected by the dense covering of leaves survive without damage. Bay is native to the Mediterranean area and was introduced into Britain by the Romans. Bay is included in the St. Gall plan, where it is called laurel. Many old gardening books refer to Bay as Laurel, and confusion has continued ever since. Parkinson lists four laurels; the Bay tree, *Laurus Tinus*, now *Viburnum tinus*; the Rose Bay, now *Nerium oleander*, *Laurocerasus*, now *Prunus laurocerasus* and finally, *Laurus Virginiana*, now called *Kalmia latifolia* which, as Parkinson comments, is neither evergreen, and nor does it have berries. The true Bay Laurel does appear to be Parkinson's favourite, not only for its use in the garden as a decorative plant, but also for its medicinal uses. He tells us that there are so many virtues to relate about the bay, that repeating them would weary the reader as much as the teller; but he repeats them anyway:

> 'It serves to adorn the house of God as well as man: to procure warmth, comfort and strength to the limes of men and women, by bathings and annoyntings outward, and by drinkes &c. inward to the stomacke, and other parts: to season vessels &c. wherein are preserved our meates, as well as our drinkes: to crowne or encircle as with a garland, the heads of the living, and to sticke and decke forth the bodies of the dead: so that from the cradle to the grave we have still use of it, we have still neede of it.'

The berries could be used to help to remove the stitches inside the body, and the external pains that come from the cold in the joints, sinews and other places. Today, bay berries are not recommended for internal use, but the essential oil of bay is often used in aromatherapy as a massage oil ingredient to help with arthritis and rheumatism, but this is not recommended for use on pregnant women as the oil has been used in the past to induce abortions.

Bay was one of the symbols of the god Apollo, who, having become enamoured of the nymph Daphne, lusted after her. One day he saw her alone and ran after her, upon which Daphne fled. As Apollo was about to catch her, Daphne who wished to preserve her chastity, called on the gods to protect her. They heeded her pleas, and she was transformed into a bay tree, as the Greek for bay is Daphne. So, very confusingly, the plant that most of us know as Daphne has nothing to do with the fabled nymph. In fond memory of the elusive maid, Apollo adopted the plant and wore a wreath of bay as a sign of his love for her.

A wreath of laurel was the prize presented to the winners at the Pythian Games, which were held every four years at Delphi, where the temple was dedicated to Apollo. There are suggestions that the oracle at Delphi induced her visons by taking a drink that included bay leaves, which if taken in large doses can be hallucinogenic. The Romans adopted the Greek custom of laurel wreaths, and the theme continues to this day. The poet laureate remembers the crowning of the best poet with a wreath of laurel. The graduate term for a batchelor, may be derived from Baccalaureate, literally berry-laurel, from the French, *Batchelier*, harking back to the time when the graduates were not allowed to marry until they had completed their studies. This term was later applied to any unmarried man.

There is an Italian liqueur called, *Liquore all'Alloro* that is made using bay leaves; the Greeks make a similar drink. Please be certain that you are using the leaves of a *Laurus nobilis*, not the leaves of Cherry Laurel, *Prunus laurocerasus*, which are poisonous:

40 crushed young bay leaves

0.5 litre vodka, or eau de vie or an equally strong, flavourless alcohol.

220g sugar. Add more or less depending on your personal preference. If you like a syrupy liqueur add more sugar.

Put the alcohol, sugar and bay leaves in a sealed container for about a month. Shake the bottle daily until the sugar has dissolved.

This is a general recipe for making a liqueur, so you can experiment with different flavours. Lemon Gin is very good. A fake anise- type drink can be made with vodka and the roots of Sweet Cicely, *Myrrhis odorata*, with no added sugar, which means that it can even be produced overnight.

All parts of the bay have been used medicinally in the past, but are no longer advised for internal use. The leaves have been used to induce sweating and vomiting. As well as inducing an abortion the berries have been used to induce the menstrual flow. Oil of Bay is still used in massage oil preparations to ease the pain of sprains and to help with bruises. It has also been poured into the ear to reduce the pain of ear ache. The leaves are often added to flavour foods such as stews, but they should be discarded after use, and not eaten.

Gerard says that common drunkards would eat two bay leaves in the morning at breakfast to prevent drunkenness. Which ties in nicely with another of his observations, that bay oil is 'good for them that be beaten blacke and blewe and that be bruised by squats and falls'.

So, useful after a rowdy night at the pub!

BINDWEED

Along with Ground Elder, Bindweed is one of the plants that most gardeners learn to hate, because even a tiny portion of root left in the soil will regenerate. The white roots can penetrate as much as 5m into the soil. In the village where I used to live, one of the Old Boys decided to trace the Bindweed roots in his allotment as deep as he could. Having spent the best part of a day at his task, he finally gave up at 2.5m. Over the years I have realised that constant hand weeding and digging out as much of the

Genus: *Calystegia*
Species: *sepium*
Family: Convolvulaceae
Other Names:
  Bindweed.
  Bellbine.
  Lady-pop-out-the-bed.
  Old Man's Nightcap.
Herbaceous Perennial
Active Constituents:
  Jalapin.
  Tannins.

root as possible will keep the bindweed under control. I had used residual weed killers, but they were not very effective and would kill any bulbs and herbaceous plants that were meant to be growing in the borders. Contact weed killers are a waste of time as they will only kill the leaves. Systemic weed killers that take the chemical down into the roots much are better, but you will still need numerous applications to control the plant, and the plant will probably still survive. Smothering the soil with old blankets

does help a little, but it only encourages the roots to find somewhere else to shoot up. Remove the covering and the bindweed will return. One method that I have never tried was described by Anne Pratt, when she was explaining how some twining plants climb in a clock-wise direction, and others twist anti-clockwise; bindweed having an anti-clockwise twist. Anne said that if the plants were trained in the wrong direction and not allowed to grow the way they naturally want to, they would perish. It may be labour intensive, but possibly worth a try.

The leaves are large and heart-shaped and with the twining stems, that will happily smother and kill anything they are allowed to grow onto. The flowers are white, large and shaped like conical trumpets, which expand as the sun becomes warmer and often refuse to even open in cold weather. Pliny made the rather odd observation that the large white bindweed grows up amongst the shrubs and that:

'It has no perfume, nor any golden anthers in the centre, yet it resembles the lily in colour, being as it were, a first attempt by Nature, when she was learning to produce lilies.'

He was correct, in some respect, as the flowers are very attractive, producing masses of bright shining blooms that glow in the sunshine, but it is best to admire them growing wild in the hedgerows, rather than introduce them into your own garden. Surprisingly, bindweed was included in a medieval plant list as something to be grown in the garden, but regardless of historical authenticity, I refused to introduce it into my gardens at the Prebendal Manor; and besides, it grew profusely in the hedges there.

Bindweed can sometimes be found with a pale pink flower, but do not be tempted to grow them at home. They are just as invasive as the white flowered plant. I saw a whole front garden in Coventry that was lost in a tangle of pink Bindweed. At one garden where I worked, the owner wanted to grow the pink flowered Bindweed, so we grew it in large pots. It was quite happy to grow up the canes we provided for the first year, but by the second year it was not thriving and escaped through the hole in the bottom of the pot. Luckily, I realised before the roots had grown into the soil.

As a child, I was shown by my mother how to gently squeeze the calyx at the base of the flower, and the flower would magically spring off, hence another common name, Lady-pop-out-the-Bed. It kept many of us amused for quite some time, but that was in the days when you had to keep yourself occupied without electronic devices to help you.

Medicinally the roots were used as a purgative as a substitute for the imported scammony, as Brook commented:

'In Northamptonshire, the poor people use the root of this plant fresh-gathered and boiled in ale as a purge; they save the expense of the apothecary, and answer the purpose better than any one thing would do for them. It would nauseate a delicate stomach, but for people of their strong constitution, there is not a better purge.'

BIRTHWORT

The botanical name comes from Greek; *aristos*, meaning best, and *lochia*, meaning birth. *Clematatis* simply means, like a clematis. The plant has a habit of spreading quickly from where it was first planted. It grows to 1.5m tall. The flowers are a yellowy green colour. The open end is flared expanding, then tapering to a point, the tubular petal tapers towards the base where there is a large, round swelling. The whole flower bears a similarity to the Cuckoo Pint, *Arum maculatum*, in miniature, but without the middle upright part. The similarity does not end there, because it employs a similar trick to the arum to attract pollinating insects, which was discovered by a German naturalist, Christian Sprengel, in 1793. Aristolochia flowers are hermaphrodite, being both female and male. They begin their development as female, when they give off a scent that is similar to rotting meat to attract flies. The flies enter the flower to reach the nectar, but become trapped by hairs that prevent their escape, but they are able to survive by eating the nectar and whilst held captive they leave pollen on the stigma. During the male phase of the flower, the insects get covered in pollen and up to two days later, the hairs wither, enabling the flies to escape and pollinate other flowers.

Genus: *Aristolochia*
Species: *clematitis*
Family: Aristolochiaceae
Other Names:
  Birthwort.
  Aristologia.
Herbaceous Perennial
Active Constituents:
  Aristolochin.
  Aristolochic acids.

Followers of the Doctrine of Signatures would say that the long tubular flowers of Birthwort suggest a similarity to the fallopian tubes and womb and that this herb could be used for problems caused by a difficult birth. Until comparatively recently in Europe, becoming pregnant and giving birth were the most dangerous things that a woman could do. Neither the status you held in life, nor the amount of wealth that you possessed would help you; the chance of dying was very high. In cases of difficult births there were birthing plants that could be used to assist an easy delivery. Most of these plants are poisonous; the mother's body would react to remove anything that threatened her life and enable her to breed later, and thus, the baby would be expelled.

Higher dosages could be used to remove the afterbirth or even a dead foetus. In very obtuse wording, the herbals suggested that even higher doses taken in early pregnancy would induce an abortion. The church certainly objected to abortions, but there must have been many women who used plants to rid themselves of an unwanted baby.

Birthwort is probably not a native plant, but it is sometimes found in the wild. It can be found growing in a hedgerow in the field that encloses the ruins of Godstow Priory. The plant grows out from underneath the central hedge and is not that noticeable until it begins to flower. The local tradition is that birthwort has grown here since the nuns used it to help the local women, and for once the tradition has a good chance of being true.

This is a plant that should not be used to self-medicate under any circumstances. It contains Aristolochic acids, that are known to cause kidney failure, and more recent research shows that taken regularly in small doses, they can lead to renal disease and cancer of the urinary tracts.

Aristolochia was also used externally, to relieve rheumatism, cuts, snake bites and venereal disease.

BLUEBELL

The English Bluebell flower stalk can grow up to 50cm, but the leaves tend to flop onto the ground. The violet blue flowers are carried on one side of the stem that gently curves towards the top. The scent given off by the flowers is powerful and sweet; some people find it quite overwhelming if they are in a good bluebell wood on a calm day. The bulbs develop contractile roots which pull the bulb deeper into the soil, which makes it difficult to dig them out of the ground. The bulbs produce

Genus: *Hyacinthoides*
Species: *non-scripta*
Family: Lilaceae
Other Names:
  Bluebell.
  Blue Bottle.
  Endymion non-scriptus.
  Scilla non-scripta.
  Endymion non-scriptus.
Bulbous Perennial
Active Constituents:
  Scillaren.

offset bulbs and seed, so they are able to multiply quite rapidly in good conditions. The bluebell should be the true flower of Saint George as it is usually in full bloom for the 23 April.

The bluebell contains poisons that are similar to the digoxin found in the foxglove, which can cause diarrhoea, nausea and vomiting. Scillaren affects the heartbeat by lowering the rate and larger doses could cause death, although there are no recorded deaths in Britain due to its ingestion, probably because bluebell bulbs are fairly small and there are no plants that can be mistaken for bluebells on any list of foods for foraging in the countryside.

A visit to a bluebell wood when the flowers are in full bloom is something that everybody should do at least once. The mass of gently nodding, soft blue flowers look like smoke from a distance, whilst a sweet perfume will scent the air. In the wild, the majority of the flowers are blue, but a white form occurs naturally, and if you are lucky you may see the occasional bluebell with pink flowers. When I was little, we would visit a local wood to pick bluebells for our Mothers. Nowadays it is best not to pick bluebells in the wild. The ones in the wood that I used to go to are perfectly safe from the locals as they are now no longer allowed to go there, but the Muntjac deer that escaped from the nearby estate Woburn Abbey where the Duke of Bedfordshire introduced them to his deer park in 1900, are very fond of bluebell leaves and will happily strip them to ground level. I planted lots of bluebells at a garden I worked at, but the Muntjac never gave them a chance. The local woodsman was given orders to keep the Muntjac under control, which he did with a relish as it gave him the chance to fill his freezer with venison. Because they are thought to be such a good garden plant, bluebells were targeted by people who were illegally digging them up from privately owned woodland without consent or any thought of leaving enough bulbs to produce plants to replace the ones that they had stolen. Eventually, the Wildlife and Countryside Act of 1981 made Hyacinthoides non-scripta a protected plant, and further legislation in 1998 made it illegal to trade in any bulbs and seed taken from the wilds. Sadly, bluebells face another equally dangerous threat, this time from another plant, the Spanish Bluebell, Hyacinthoides hispanica, which was introduced as a garden plant during the seventeenth century. The Spanish bluebell has escaped from being confined in the garden and is now cross-breeding with the native bluebell to produce vigorous hybrids that can rapidly replace *Hyacinthoides non-scripta*.

It is easy to tell the two species apart in their pure form. *Hyacinthoides non-scripta* has leaves that are 1 to 1.5cm wide, whilst *Hyacinthoides hispanica* has leaves that are about 3cm wide. The native bluebell has a stem that hangs over slightly at the end, with the sweetly scented flowers mostly growing from only one side. The tubular ends of the petals curl back on themselves. The stem of the Spanish bluebell is broader and stands erect with the flowers, which have little or no scent, will grow from all sides. The flowers are more conical than the native bluebell and the ends of the petals flare out. The pollen of the native bluebell is white; that of the Spanish bluebell is blue.

The bluebell does not appear in Dioscorides, nor any other old herbal that was written by the ancient Greeks or Romans, because it does not occur naturally in southern Europe, growing mostly in western Europe. Later herbalists tried to associate it with the south European hyacinth. Gerard had very little to say about the bluebell other than that it could be used to make a glue.

According to Greek myth, Hyakinthos was a beautiful youth who caught the attention of the god Apollo, who fell in love with him and the two spent much time together in manly pursuits. The West Wind Zephyrus also fell in love with Hyakinthos and became very jealous of Apollo's attentions to the youth. One day, Apollo and Hyakinthos were throwing the discus, much as children today play with a Frisbee, each taking turns to throw the discus for the other to catch. As Apollo threw the discus, Zephyrus in a fit of rage took a deep breath and blew a gust of wind at the discus as Hyakinthos was about to catch it. The youth failed to catch the discus, which hit him on the forehead, killing him. Apollo was distraught and full of grief. He refused to let Hades claim his lover, so he turned him into the flower, but as Apollo wept, his tears stained the petals with the words of his grief, *Al. Al*, meaning' *Alas. Alas*, but in Greek of course, and the flower became known as the hyacinth. So, to this day, the Hyacinth of southern Europe bears the same words, but the west European one does not, so it is *non-scriptus*, literally a hyacinth-like plant but 'without the words'.

BROOM

Broom is a shrub that prefers to grow on open heath, reaching a height of 3m. It has long spindly branches with trifoliate leaves. The yellow pea-like flowers have a very sweet scent, which can be over powering where there are lots of plants growing together. The flowers begin to bloom in April and continue through May. The seed cases look similar to small pea pods, ripening from green to black, containing round seeds. On a hot dry day, you will hear the ripening pods opening with loud cracking noises, like a series of gun shots, as they scatter the seeds.

Genus: *Cytisus*
Species: *scoparius*
Family: Fabaceae
Other Names:
   Common Broom.
   Broom.
Evergreen Shrub
Active Constituents:
   Sparteine.

The Plantagenet dynasty are traditionally said to have taken their name from Planta genista, because of the habit of Count Geoffrey of Anjou, the father of King Henry II of England, who wore a sprig of broom in his hat. Another theory is that the family originally began life as gardeners, before working their way into power. A more recent theory suggests the name came from the habit of the male line to father many children, legitimate or otherwise, to ensure a large family that could be drawn on for political support. Broom has now become another name for a brush, or a besom, which was made of a bundle of twigs attached to a handle. The plant used to make the brush head varies according to which part of the country they are made in. In some areas it is heather, others birch and some it really was made of the common broom plant. A good besom broom is still the best tool for sweeping turf. The whippy stems were used by gardeners instead of twine to tie plants to supports. Broom rape is a parasitic plant that grows on the roots of broom. Gerard said that it grew in a field of broom at Shooters Hill, close to London on Hampstead heath. Broom rape was used in medicine by extracting the juice to clean old ulcerous wounds; or it could be boiled in wine and drunk to ease kidney pains and to induce urine. Broom rape could be used cosmetically by macerating it and then soaking it in olive oil for a few days; it was used to remove spots, freckles and pimples from the face or any other part of the body. The Syon Herbal gave a recipe for an ointment containing broom to be used externally for general aches. Olive oil, bees wax and turpentine were to be melted together, add the juice of rue, the juice of broom flowers and bramble tops, boil together and store in a glass for later use. The flower buds could be pickled or laid in salt, and after washing could be eaten in salads like capers. Or you could mash them into pig fat to make an ointment for gout. Broom was a diuretic and known as *Scroparii Cacuminal*, by the apothecary.

According to Gerard:

'That woorthie Prince of famous memorie Henrie the eight of England was woont to drinke the distilled water of Broome flowers against surfets and diseases thereof arising.'

Henry would have especially needed broom in his medicine chest during his later years. A decoction of the stems and tips were good to remove the watery humours by stool or as a vomit, or bruised and steeped in water for use with sciatica and quinsy. Broom was a purge, but not so dangerous as hellebore, because you were less likely to die as a result of taking it.

CAPER SPURGE

The Caper Spurge is an attractive, branching plant growing to 1.5m. The leaves are arranged like crosses of four up the stems and are a glaucous colour with prominent white midribs and veins. If you break a leaf or any other part of the plant, a milky white sap will soon appear. The flowers are a green/yellow colour, followed by seed cases of the same colour as the leaves which gradually fade and become paler. The

Genus: *Euphorbia*
Species: *lathyris*
Family: Euphorbiaceae
Other Names:
    Caper Spurge.
    Mole Plant.
    Catapuce.
Biennial/Annual
Active Constituents:
    Aesculetin.

seed cases partly resemble those of capers, but they are not the true caper, so pickling and eating the seed cases will have rather unfortunate results. If a plant is called a spurge, it is a purge, and this one is a very powerful purge. All parts of the plant are poisonous.

Caper spurge often arrives in gardens where it has never grown before, as if by magic, having been introduced by birds. Some gardening books, articles and personalities still pass on the information that it is called the Mole Plant and will drive moles away from your garden. Wrong type of moles! Somebody misunderstood the old herbals which say that it can be used to remove moles; those on the skin! The sap of euphorbias can cause blistering on the skin, so may well remove moles too. A vinegar made with the root of spurge was used as a cosmetic to remove severe scabies from the face.

I once saw the effect of the sap on a gardener's arm. He had been pruning out the flowered stems of *Euphorbia characiassubsp.Wulfenii*, by reaching through the bottom of the plants to cut out the stems at ground level. As he did so, he was knocking off some of the lower leaves allowing the sap to run. The inside of his lower arm appeared to have been burned with a hot poker laid across the skin from the wrists upwards. Since then I have been more careful myself as the inside of the arm is more tender than the outside and more susceptible to being affected.

The caper spurge has a long history of use as a medicine to balance the humours. Seeds were found during the excavation of the Roman villa at Bancroft in Milton Keynes. It is likely that the plant was being deliberately grown for medicinal use. This was probably a dangerous medicine as during the medieval period Arderne wrote that you should not give euphorbias to a patient as an oral medicine because of its strength.

In Chaucer's story of the Nun's Priests Tale, Chanticleer the cockerel has been having bad dreams. His wife Pertelote suggests that the dreams have been caused by an imbalance of humours and says that he needs to take some laxatives, which included caper spurge, to bring his humours back into balance which would stop his nightmares. Unfortunately for Chanticleer, his bad dreams did come true when through his vanity he was caught by a fox, but at least he survived and learned to resist flattery. Hildegard quite rightly said that the plant was not very useful in medicine because it is poisonous and will burn the flesh, which makes one wonder why anybody would want to try a recipe contained in the *Trotula* to induce sexual arousal in men. Take the dry seeds of caper spurge and crush them into a fine powder. Mix the powder with musk and pennyroyal oils and anoint the loins. This is definitely not something that I would want to try.

Gerard told of an occasion when he and his friend, Mr Lee, both tasted a single drop of the juice of this spurge, which caused a burning and swelling in their throats, so much so, that Gerard said he was in fear of his life. They quickly mounted their horses and rode to a nearby farm to drink some milk which reduced the heat. From this personal experience, Gerard recommended that you should not take the plant internally, especially as there were so many safe alternatives.

Caper spurge could be used as a cosmetic to remove unwanted hair by mixing the juice with honey and rubbing it onto the skin in sunlight, which if you were not careful could result with blistered skin, rather than soft, silky, smooth skin.

If you were in need of a quick meal and wanted fish, you could catch them very swiftly by mixing the spurge with anything that the fish eat. Throw the mixture into the water and very soon the fish would float to the surface.

CASTOR OIL PLANT

The castor oil plant originates from the Mediterranean area, the Middle East, North Africa and India. In areas that do not have frosts, the plant is an evergreen tree growing to heights of 12m, but in Britain it is grown as an annual from seed every year, although it can be over-wintered in a warm greenhouse. The leaves vary in colour from dark green to a deep red/purple. They are palmate, deeply cut and can be up to 50cm wide. Gerard called the plant *Palma Christi*,

Genus: *Ricinis*
Species: *communis*
Family: Euphorbiaceae
Other Names:
    Castor Oil Plant.
    Palma Christi.
    Kik.
Evergreen Tender Perennial/Annual
Active Constituents:
    Ricin.

because the leaf looks like an open hand and Dioscorides said that the name *ricinus* was used because the seed looks like a tick of the same name. They have insignificant flowers, with both male and female on the same plant. The seed case is like a small conker that can be green, pink or bright red. The red leaf forms, with a pink or red seedcase, are very attractive for floral arrangements. The plants were very popular in bedding schemes to give a tropical effect. The Victorians were fond of the plants with red or purple coloured leaves. It was suggested that if you found a good coloured plant, you should keep it carefully so that the seeds were more likely to give you similar plants in future. Some of the seeds can be beautifully marked and in the past, they have been used to make necklaces. With the popularity of foreign holidays in the early 1970s, people visiting Tenerife often bought such necklaces to take back home for nieces and other young girls. I remember reading a newspaper article about how a sharp-eyed customs official realised that some of the seeds were from the castor oil plant. Young girls who wear necklaces often suck and chew the beads, and this could have been fatal; it only needs four to eight seeds to kill an adult. Even as recently as 2015, the Eden Project imported bracelets made of the bright red seeds of the Rosary Pea – which were quickly withdrawn from sale as they could have proved equally fatal. The oil obtained from the seed, Cicinum, was known poisonous and not to be eaten, because it was 'harsh and extremely laboursome, mightily overturning the stomach'; so it was used to make candles, plaster and was good for sunburn, or even rubbed onto the body to remove roughness caused by the itch.

Eating the seed would open the belly and cause vomit to remove slimy filth, whilst a broth of water in which the seeds had been soaked was good for gout, sciatica, jaundice and dropsy. Castor oil was a common laxative, even into the early 1960s. People of a certain age, will remember that as children, on a Friday evening we were often given a spoonful to clean out our insides.

The most famous incident of ricin being used as a poison for murder was when Georgi Markov, the dissident Bulgarian journalist was murdered in 1978 on Waterloo Bridge in London when a ricin-laced poison pellet was injected into his leg from an umbrella. Following the London bombings of Thursday, 7 July 2005, when fifty-two people were killed and over seven hundred were injured, the seeds of *Ricinis communis* were taken off the market in the UK, as it was feared that terrorists would be able to process the seeds to make ricin and potentially use it to poison reservoirs. The process must be more difficult than was first thought, as the seeds are now available again.

CELANDINE, GREATER

There is only one species of *Chelidonium*. It is a member of the poppy family, and if you look closely at the leaves you can see a certain similarity to those of the field poppy. Greater celandine tends to be found growing at the base of walls and waste areas. If you knock the plant during June and July you will disturb large clouds of whitefly. Greater celandine is an erect, bushy plant that can reach 1.20m. The pinnate leaves are lobed and have a glaucous colour. The yellow flowers are borne on cymes, usually four flowers on each. Each individual flower has four petals and two sepals; a multi-petalled form is often grown as a garden plant. The black seeds are contained in long thin pods of a cylindrical section.

Genus: *Chelidonium*
Species: *majus*
Family: Papaveraceae
Other Names:
   Greater Celandine.
   Salandine.
   Wartweed.
   Swallow Wort.
   Yellow Spit.
   Tetter Wort.

Herbaceous Perennial

Active Constituents:
   Chelidonine.
   Chelerythrine.
   Homochelidonine.
   Coptisine.
   Berberine.
   Sanguinarine.

The seed has an external growth on it that ants like to feed on called an elaiosome; the plant is really taking advantage of the ants, as they help to disperse its seed. The ants carry the seeds back to their nests where the elaiosome is kept for food; the seeds are of no use to them, so the ants take them to an area where they dispose of their waste, and if conditions are suitable, the seeds can then germinate.

If you break the stem you will see a yellow sap. This can stain your fingers and has been used in the past to remove warts and moles from the skin. I have met people who have tried this and claimed that it worked. Commercial products are available for the same use. The sap has a peculiar scent and has a sharp taste.

Chelidonium is a Greek word for a swallow. Dioscorides said that the plant was said to have acquired the name as it begins to flower when the swallows return for the summer and starts to wither when the swallows depart. Sadly, there seem to be fewer swallows returning every year, but the celandine still grows much the same as ever. There is another connection with the swallow. Dioscorides wrote that the female swallow would cure the blindness of her chicks in the nest by dropping the sap of the plant into their eyes. The story was recounted by Pliny, Crescenzi and others; but Gerard discounted the story as vain and false, but then said that if the eyes of the young swallows were picked out before they fledged, they would grow back again and their sight would be restored. He then went on to recommend that celandine could be boiled with honey to remove slime and other matter from the eye ball.

This ancient use of celandine continued to be used to clear the eyesight and to remove cloudiness and films on the eyes, for both humans and animals. A.A. Forsyth, who in 1954 wrote a government booklet on poisonous plants, said that he had been called out several times to treat cattle and horses with conjunctivitis as a result of having their eyes bathed with greater celandine, which shows how long some of traditional herb lore has continued to be followed.

Greater celandine was also one of the many cures for snake bites, often taken in wine, which probably helped to hide the bitter taste, but would also be safe to drink, which the water may not have been. Gerard, in his usual droll manner, said that the root could be cut into small pieces and fed to hawks against the sundry diseases to which they were prone. Hawks were a symbol of a high status because they needed such a lot of care, and only the wealthy could afford to pay for it.

Celandine was used to strengthen loose teeth by boiling the root in vinegar, or you could chew the root mixed with vinegar to reduce toothache. Scrofulous sores, suppurations and wounds could be relieved by celandine mixed with axle grease and honey, or mixed with wine it could be used to wipe away spots and freckles. John Arderne gave a recipe for an ointment that he said he would never be without. It was called Salus Populi, and greater celandine was one of the main ingredients.

Equal amounts of celandine and nearly as much ivy were crushed together and added to harts, or sheep tallow and half as much olive oil. They were heated together until the mixture became black, then poured into a container to cool and harden. When needed for use, a quantity of it should be put in an oyster shell and heated over a candle. It was rubbed around open wounds or used on burns, or on lips burned by the sun or wind. It could be rubbed onto the hands, legs and feet and was also one of the best remedies for haemorrhoids.

According to the Doctrine of Signatures, the yellow sap hinted at as a cure for jaundice, and many herbals do use the plant for this purpose.

CELANDINE, LESSER

You can tell that Spring is on its way when the star-like golden flowers of the lesser celandine sparkle in the sunshine. They can usually be seen from late February in Britain, but by mid-May the leaves are turning yellow and the plant disappears from view. It grows to 5cm and prefers a damp shady area, shining like a beacon in the hedgerows, along the roadsides and much to the dismay of many gardeners, in

Genus: *Ranunculus*
Species: *ficaria*
Family: Ranunculaceae
Other Names:
 Lesser Celandine.
 Pilewort. Lesser
 Figwort.
Herbaceous Perennial
Active Constituents:
 Protoanemonin

lawns and flower beds. Wordsworth must have been impressed with the celandines as wrote three poems about them; The Small Celandine, To the Same Flower and To the Small Celandine.

The leaves are dark green and heart shaped which can, if crushed in contact with the skin, cause blisters, itching and rashes. The roots have small tubers, like miniature potatoes; leave one in the ground as you try to remove the plant and you will have another plant in its place the following year. If you indiscriminately spread the soil as you are digging, the tubers will be dispersed too and the celandine will show its face in places that you were not expecting. The other main method of spreading is from tubercles, small bulbils, that form where the leaf joins the stem; and lastly, it can also set seed in a good year. This is a plant that is determined to succeed. In one garden that I worked in we decided to let the celandines remain underneath a magnolia, as nothing else would grow there. It was not too difficult to prevent them escaping … most of the time. It is this ability to reproduce rapidly that has led the United States of America to list the lesser celandine as a plant pest of gardens and natural areas, because since 2014 it has established itself in twenty-five states; potentially threatening the survival of endangered native plants.

The Doctrine of Signatures suggests what the roots could be used to cure. The root tubers are meant to look like haemorrhoids, otherwise known as piles. I am forced to take the herbals' word for it, having never suffered from them myself. Piles were also called figs, hence the name figwort. There is another plant called figwort for the same reason, *Scrophularia nodosa*, which is a tall plant that grows near water. A cream made with the root tubers of the lesser celandine was said to ease the pain of the afflicted person.

If you would love to see this herald of spring in your own garden, but cannot face the thought of being over-run by them, there is a cultivar with bronze-coloured leaves, which is suitably named as, 'Brazen Hussy'. The flowers contrast well against the dark leaves, and luckily, she does not spread quite so rapidly as her wild relative.

CHERRY LAUREL

The Cherry laurel can become a small tree, growing to a height of 15m, although it is usually grown for hedging and rarely allowed to grow to its full height. The leaves are a dark shiny green on the upper surface, and can have a slight scent of almonds when bruised. In May, sweetly scented, creamy white flowers are produced on racemes. The cherry sized fruit is black when it is fully ripe. The species part of the botanical name means a laurel like a cherry, referring to the berries. Cherry laurel grows naturally in Albania, the Balkans, Iran, Turkey, South East Europe and south-western Asia and was introduced into England as a garden plant from Constantinople in 1576 by Clusius, who in turn had received it from David Ungnad, the Ambassador to the Emperor of Constantinople. Parkinson said that he received his plant as a gift from Master John Cole, a London merchant who loved to grow rare plants, who had a fine cherry laurel at his home in Highgate that he cautiously protected from frosts by covering it with a blanket. Nowadays, we know that cherry laurel is not so delicate.

Although we tend to disdain it now, the laurel was once prized for its

Genus: *Prunus*
Species: *laurocerasus*
Family: Rosaceae
Other Names:
Laurel.
Cherry Laurel.
Hardy Evergreen Tree/ Shrub
Active Constituents:
Cyanolipids.

glossy evergreen leaves, there being few native evergreens in Britain. It gave a bright green edging to paths, protecting people in the garden from the heat of the sun during the summer and from the cold, winter winds. Thomas Hanmer said that the tree was well known in North Wales, being grown against walls, as standards and in arbours and palisades, being more useful than the bay tree because it was better able to withstand the cold weather without damage. He added that laurel was used indoors in pots and as a backing for the smaller flowers in nosegays, as it still is used by florists today.

Bitter almonds were the main source of cyanide, a poison that was popular with both gardeners and murderers. Most people have seen at least one old murder-mystery film where the detective leans over the face of the dead victim's face, takes a sniff and says, 'Almonds. It was cyanide'. But cyanide can be found in many other plants too. During the Victorian and Edwardian periods men of leisure collected insects and pinned them onto boards. How do you kill and insect without damaging it? You crush laurel leaves, put them in a jar, drop in the insect and fix an airtight lid on it. Very soon the insect will have died of cyanide poisoning. This method for killing insects is still being described on the internet. A similar, but more practical use for in the garden was suggested by Shirley Hibbard, when he recommended that laurel water was very effective for killing any caterpillars that you found on your cabbages. Laurel water was used medicinally as a mild narcotic sedative, being known as, *Aqua Laurocerasi*, by the apothecary, but it is no longer used. The instructions to make the water were very simple:

'One pound (500g) of laurel leaves chopped and pounded in a mortar.
Two and a half pints (1.75l) of water.
Add the crushed leaves to the water and let it stand for twenty-four hours. Distil the liquid to take off one pint of the water, then filter it to remove impurities before storing in a clean sealed bottle. One drop of sulphuric acid could be added to the water to help it keep for longer, but generally the distilled water should be replaced after a year.'

At a recent talk a member of the audience told me of a drink that they had been given in France in the early part of this century. The recipe used fifty laurel leaves, which were cut up and put into *eau de vie* with some sugar and left for a few months to allow the flavour to soak into the alcohol. She remembered that the drink was quite tasty but she had wondered why it was not poisonous. I asked if it was in fact the recipe had used bay tree leaves, because bay is often referred to as laurel, but she told me that she had seen the drink being made; it was definitely cherry laurel leaves! I would certainly not recommend the drink. I think that the person making it had misunderstood the recipe because the drink should be made with bay leaves. I hope that the person in France who used the cherry laurel leaves did not suffer any ill-effects, especially in view of the following report. *Taylors Principle and Practice of Medical Jurisprudence* reported a case of a fatal poisoning after somebody drank the first glass from a bottle of *Crème de Noyaux,* a liqueur flavoured with hazelnuts. The author reported that enough prussic acid, another name for cyanide, to kill a person had accumulated in the bottle and floated to the top.

The 'Teacup Murderer', Graham Young claimed to have murdered a fellow inmate, John Berridge, by extracting cyanide from the cherry laurel that was growing in the garden whilst they were both patients at Broadmoor Hospital. Young had begun to experiment at an early age, when he was still at school. He poisoned members of his family with various poisons, including antimony. He attempted to poison his sister, Winfred, in November 1961, by putting atropa belladonna in her tea. She only drank a little and threw the rest away because of the bitter taste, but she had still drunk enough to make her hallucinate on the bus to work. Graham denied that he was to blame, saying that Winifred had been mixing shampoo in the teacup. On Easter Saturday the following year, Young's stepmother, Molly died from poisoning. Suspicions were aroused. Young was sent to a psychiatrist, who then involved the police. On 23 May 1962, Young was arrested and later confessed to the attempted murders of his father, sister, and a school friend. The police could not press charges for the murder of Molly as she had been cremated. Young was sent to Broadmoor Hospital under the Mental Health Act, where he remained until 1971, apparently cured of his obsession with poisons. He soon managed to find work at the John Hadland Laboratories in Bovingdon, Hertfordshire. Soon after he began work, a sickness that the workers nicknamed the Bovingdon Bug, began to affect the workers. Bob Egle, Young's foreman died and sometime after another work colleague, Fred Biggs died after a protracted illness; another seventy people had been made ill. Sadly, Young's employers had not been made aware of his interest in poisons. Young was arrested on 21 November 1971. Police later found thallium in his pocket, and aconitine, antimony and thallium were discovered in his home, along with a diary that recorded the doses of poison that he was administering to his work mates. Young was later tried and found guilty of murder and attempted murder. He remained in prison until he died just before his forty third birthday on 1 August 1990 at Parkhurst Prison.

There are many tales on the internet about people who have become ill from chipping laurel branches or loading clippings into the back of a car to take to the local tip. It is now being recommended that you do not burn the pruning waste of Laurel.

CHINESE LANTERNS

Chinese lanterns grow to 60cm tall. The dark green leaves can be 12cm long and 9cm across the widest part; they are arranged in a spiral around the stem. The flowers have five petals that are white with a green/yellow tinge. Later, the orange lanterns form, up to 5cm. long; within which you will find a large red/orange, juicy berry that has a bitter taste. The berries are not the physalis that you buy at the supermarket for use in fruit salads. I have known people who ate the berries, but some sources suggest that they are poisonous, especially if not fully ripe, when they may cause diarrhoea, headache, stomach ache, vomiting, dilated pupils and breathing problems. Eating the leaves will have the same effects. The roots are thick and white with a rapidly spreading habit.

Genus: *Physalis*
Species: *alkekengi*
Family: Solanaceae
Other Names:
  Chinese Lanterns.
  Winter Cherry.
Herbaceous Perennial
Active Constituents:
  Hygrine.
  Tigloyloxy-tropane.
  Physalin A, B, and
  C. Solanine.

Chinese Lanterns were one of the ubiquitous plants of my childhood. Everybody in the village grew them – mostly because they spread rapidly and needed controlling, so the spare roots were passed on to your neighbours, who passed them on, until everybody in the village had a clump. Now the plant's popularity has decreased and it is rarely seen in either gardens or garden centres.

Alkengii was included in Charlemagne's, *Capitulari de Villis*, a list he had drawn up to ensure that all his estates were properly maintained and stocked. The list included all the plants that Charlemagne considered to be essential, and which should be grown on his estates; unfortunately for us it is only a list, as none of the intended uses were included. Dioscorides said that the leaves could be used to cure jaundice, stops a woman's period, and mixed with bread would help *aegilops*, an ulcer or fistula in the inner corner of the eye. The juice mixed with yellow dung from hens kept in a barn was also a remedy for *aegilops*. The lanterns look like bladders, so under the Doctrine of Signatures, the plant must be connected with urinary problems, so it was often used for breaking kidney stones and for other kidney diseases. For once, one of the recipe sounds quite palatable:

'Bruise the berries and infuse or steep them in white wine for two or three hours, then bring them to the boil for two or three bubblings; strain the liquid, then add sugar and cinnamon.'

The drink was mainly intended for urinary problems, but it could also be taken for jaundice.

As a Head Gardener, I had a safer use for the plant. I would allow the lanterns to become fully formed and cut the stems at ground level. Then I removed all the leaves and allowed the lanterns to dry on the stems by standing them in an empty jar. The dried stems could be used for winter floral decoration with other dried seed heads and flowers. I had another way of using them; I would cut off the individual lanterns, leaving a short stem, around which I wrapped some thin florists wire so that I could add them to wreaths, table displays and other seasonal decorations. In a moist autumn, the outer casing of the lantern itself will often slightly rot away, leaving what has often described as a coin in a net purse. The effect is very attractive and popular with flower arrangers. Not all autumns are suitably moist for the process to occur naturally. Some internet sites describe how to remove the outer casing by dipping the individual lanterns into a caustic soda solution. If you don't wear gloves you will have a slippery, soapy feeling on your fingers; it is your skin starting to disintegrate. If you do decide to try using the caustic soda, please wear gloves and preferably eye protection.

CORN COCKLE

Corncockle is one of the plants that once commonly grew amongst the corn, along with other plants such as poppies, cornflowers and corn marigolds, and it probably arrived in Britain amongst the grain brought by travellers or colonisers. The name of the plant is well chosen, agros refers to fields and stemma means a wreath; literally the plant that decorates the fields with its bright cerise flowers that are

Genus: *Agrostemma*
Species: *githago*
Family: Caryophyllaceae
Other Names:
    Corncokle.
    Cockle.
    Gith.
Hardy Annual
Active Constituents:
    Githagin.

3.5cm in diameter. It can grow to over 1m tall. Sadly, the seeds contain an oil which would send the flour rancid if the seeds were milled with the grain; but the oil is also poisonous. Each plant can produce about three hundred or more seeds. The seeds remain in their cases unless they are broken or rotten, so that in the past, the seeds easily became mixed in with the grain, to later contaminate the flour with their toxic oil. Herbivores are less affected than carnivores, and chickens are thought to be immune to the githagin. The efficient sieving of the grain to remove the seeds and modern pesticides has ensured that corncockles are unlikely to be seen in the wild again. The seeds are the most poisonous part of the plant and can cause stomach pains and diarrhoea. In severe cases, the red blood cells may be destroyed, with death resulting from heart and breathing failure.

Gerard wrote that:

'What hurt it doth among corne, the spoile of bread, as well in colour, taste and unwholesomnesse, is better known than desired.'

Other herbalists said that corncockle was good for promoting urine and the menses and helped jaundice and dropsy, but corncockles are no longer used medicinally.

I discovered just how poisonous the seeds are by accident. I had collected the dry seed cases of corncockle from an area of wild flowers that I had been growing in a medieval garden. I crushed the seed cases in a pan and carefully blew the husks away and poured the seeds into trays to leave them overnight to make sure they had dried properly. The next morning, I returned to the potting shed to see some of the seeds had been scattered and there were mouse droppings – but there were no more signs of mice for the rest of the winter.

The flower is well worth growing in the garden, being no more dangerous than many other garden plants and the seed is readily available. You can obtain a white flowered variety, but I still prefer the cerise flowers.

DAFFODIL

The daffodil is probably one of the best-known flowers to herald the Spring, although more recently they have become confused by the warming climate and have been recorded as flowering in December. Because it is one of the earliest flowers, the daffodil was associated with new beginnings and rebirth in the language of flowers. The daffodil, *Narcissus pseudonarcissus* is a native plant in Britain, and can still be seen in the western parts of Britain much as

Genus: *Narcissus*
Species: *pseudonarcissus*
Family: Amarylidaceae
Other Names:
  Daffodil.
  Lent Lily.
  Daffy-Down-Dilly.
Perennial Bulb
Active Constituents:
Galantamine. Lycorine.
Scillitoxin.

Gerard had remarked. These are the flowers that brought such ecstasy to Wordsworth and inspired Shakespeare to include them in several poems, where he called them daffy-down-dillies.

The native daffodil is a much smaller plant than the cultivars bred by the nurserymen and there are many other introduced species that are grown in gardens. The species name, pseudonarcissus, goes back to older definitions when people such as Parkinson said that the true narcissus had a trumpet that was short and not as long as the flower was wide. So, the other 'bastard daffodils', as they were called, were all false narcissi, and thus named as pseudo. In fact, many of the plants listed as daffodils by earlier writers were not true narcissi at all. The plant that Parkinson named as the, 'Strange Sea Daffodil', is an Agapanthus and Gerard calls the Snake's-Head Fritillary a daffodil too. Such confusion was not new. The Agnus Castus herbal says that:

> 'Affadilla is an herb that men call Affadille or belle bloom. It is like a leek, and has a yellow flower and in the seed pod there are seeds that are like onion seed. The leaves are good to heal dropsy and help with the bites of venomous worms. The juice mixed with myrrh, saffron simmered in sweet wine is good for running sores. The bulb can be powdered and rubbed onto the scalp as a hair restorer.'

The only problem is that the name and description could apply equally well to both the yellow asphodel, *Aspodeline lutea,* or the daffodil.

According to Ovid in his *Metamorphoses*, Narcissus was an attractive youth who enjoyed hunting. One day while he was hunting a deer, Echo, a nymph, saw him and immediately fell in love with him. Echo had fallen foul of Hera, the wife of the king of the gods, Zeus. Hera had placed a curse on Echo, so that she could only repeat what others had spoken. Narcissus spurned Echo's advances. Echo prayed to Aphrodite, who magically allowed Echo's body to disappear, leaving only her voice behind. Meanwhile, Narcissus had tired of hunting and rested by a pool, where he took a drink. As he leaned over the pool for refreshment, he suddenly saw a the most beautiful face peering back at him. He instantly fell in love with the face, and sat entranced by the vision of beauty; so much so that he could not leave and slowly he died from love. Some say it was poetic justice for his spurning of Echo's love for him. In his place the narcissus flower grew, nodding gently over the pool where the youth had died.

Pliny had another explanation for the narcissus part of the plant name. His reason is that it was derived from the word, *Narcao*, which is a Greek word meaning 'to become numb' because of the plants ability to cause numbness. The scent of the Poet's narcissus in an enclosed space has been said to cause headaches and vomiting in some people.

If you grow daffodils in your garden, do not chop the leaves off after the flowers have died, nor tie them in knots or many of the other things people do to try to make them look tidier. The plants need to be able to photosynthesise properly to build up their energy for the next spring. If you want to cut the grass and do not want to leave the daffodils to spoil the scenery, grow the dwarf species as the leaves will die down more quickly. In a flower border, it is best to grow the spring flowers towards the back so that the summer flowering plants will hide the dying foliage from view. Some books recommend removing the dead flower heads so that the energy the plants produce will go back to the bulb, rather than in producing seed. This is fine if you only have a few daffodils, but not if you have masses of them. Many of the Narcissi have good scents. I used to grow several bowls of 'Paperwhite' in succession to provide the house with a continual scented display over the winter months.

Theophrastus and Dioscorides both mention *Narcissus poeticus*, the poet's narcissus. This is the plant that was said to have been introduced to his garden in Findern, Derbyshire by Geoffrey de Fynderne on his return from the Crusades. It is still known locally as the Findern Lily. The bulb of the daffodil has been eaten having been mistaken for an onion. Only a few years ago supermarkets were forced by Public Health England to display their daffodil bulbs further away from the cash tills in an attempt to stop people picking them up instead of onions. How anybody could think that a daffodil bulb is an onion is still beyond me; surely the lack of a strong onion-smell would be a good indicator?

However, poisoning from daffodils is not something to be discounted lightly. All parts of the plant are toxic, although the bulb is the most dangerous part, and heat does not seem to destroy the toxic properties. You do not need to eat many of the bulbs and the poison is fast acting. The poison leads to nausea, diarrhoea, stomach ache and vomiting. In very severe cases it can cause collapse and then death through paralysis of the central nervous system.

Extracts from Narcissi can be useful in modern medicine. Galantamine extracted from narcissi bulbs has been used to treat Alzheimer's dementia.

DAPHNE LAUREOLA

A native evergreen that usually lurks unseen in hedgerows, but can be found in woodland, where it can grow to 1.2m. The leaves are dark green and very shiny and tend to be fewer on the lower parts of the stems. The stems can be erect or flop and then grow up again. If the branches remain in contact with the soil they can take root, so the plant can be propagated by layering or grown from seed. The scented yellow flowers

Genus: *Daphne*
Species: *laureola*
Family: Thymelaeaceae
Other Names:
 Spurge Laurel.
 Laureola.
Evergreen Shrub
Active Constituents:
 Daphnin.
 Coumarin.

appear in late winter and early spring, depending on weather conditions, and later in the Spring there will be black berries. Inexperienced gardeners often mistake the plant for one of the euphorbias as it has a similar growth habit.

Although commonly called a laurel, it not related to any other plant that is called a laurel. Likewise, it is not related to the spurge, *Euphorbia*; the spurge in this instance is referring to purging, because in the past the bark was mostly used as a purge. It was said to be good to clear phlegm. All parts of the plant are poisonous, including the sap which can cause rashes on the skin; something which it does have in common with Euphorbia. It was as a purge that the plant was mostly used for throughout history, and Coles noted one tradition that claimed that if you broke off a branch upwards, then the resulting purging would be a vomit and if broken off with a downwards motion the purge would also be downwards. Pharmacists once sold the bark of daphne as a purge, naming it *Cortex Mezerei*. The bark of either *Daphne mezereum* or *Daphne laureola*, was allowed to be used, as there was little difference in the purging effect between either of them.

DAPHNE MEZEREUM

aphne mezereum is the daphne that most people recognise. It is probably an introduced plant. It is a slow growing shrub, reaching 1.5m and has small, very sweetly scented purple flowers, which is why people grow it; the flowers appear in early spring before the leaves. The red berries are poisonous, as is the rest of the plant to humans, although some birds can eat the berries without any ill-effect. As mentioned in *Daphne laureola*, the bark, *Cortex Mezerei*, was used as a purge. Handling the stems has caused rashes in some cases. Dioscorides said that Daphne mezereum induced vomiting or purging, which continued to be its main use for centuries. It provoked the menstrual flow, which Pliny agreed with, but he added that it could be taken to remove the afterbirth. As a purge, he said that fifteen berries were to be taken, which sounds rather drastic.

Genus: *Daphne*
Species: *mezereum*
Family: Thymelaeaceae
Other Names:
    Daphne.
    Mezereon.
Deciduous Shrub
Active Constituents:
    Mezerein.
    Daphnin.
    Coumarin.

Pechey, an eighteenth-century doctor, said that mezereum burned the mouth, jaws and throat but was very good to purge Choler. He said that the plant should be corrected by soaking in either vinegar or wine and then drying it again. Both methods would work, but he went on to warn that:

> 'the leaves, bark, or berries, howsoever they are prepared and corrected, are seldom used, by reason of their malignity: Nor, indeed, ought they to be used, but in desperate Cases, or for want of safer medicines.'

Mezereum could also lead to bloody stools, which with Pechey's warning is surely enough to explain why the use of *Daphne mezereum* as a medicine has been discontinued.

DEADLY NIGHTSHADE

The true deadly nightshade is often confused with woody nightshade, which has purple flowers with pointed yellow centres and scrambles in hedgerows and across wasteland. Deadly nightshade is an herbaceous perennial that grows to 2m then dies down over winter. It prefers to grow in moist, shady woodland. It is not common in most parts of the country, although I once walked through the woods close to Arundel Castle where deadly nightshade grew in prolific abundance.

Genus: *Atropa*
Species: *belladonna*
Family: Solanáceae
Other Names:
  Belladonna.
  Devil's Cherries.
  Dwale.
  Sleeping Nightshade.
Herbaceous Perennial
Active Constituents:
  Atropine.
  Hyoscyamine.
  Belladonnine.
  Scopolamine.

My own plants originated from a vicar's garden which I was redesigning. I found a Deadly Nightshade plant growing in one of the borders. I told the vicar's wife, who asked me to dig it up before the grandchildren visited later that day. I potted the plant and took it home to propagate more plants as I had not found a plant locally until then.

The tubular flowers, which are about 25mm in length, are a murky shade of purple, which seems very suitable for a poisonous plant. The berries are the size of a cherry and have a very shiny surface, even when they are still green. I have several photographs where my reflection is clearly visible on the berries. Gerard agreed with this observation and remarked that Deadly Nightshade has:

'A berry of a bright shining black colour and of such great beauty as it were, to allure any such to eat thereof.'

Unlike most poisonous plants, the berries are sweet; making it very easy for a child to eat the ten berries which could be fatal. I have tested the juice on my tongue, so I can vouch that the berries do have a sweet taste.

Gerard told a story of three boys from Wisbech who had eaten deadly nightshade berries and become very ill; two of them died within eight hours. The third boy, who was made to vomit by drinking water and honey mixed together, survived. Gerard was most forthright in stating that you should not allow the plant to grow in your gardens or even nearby, where children may find the berries. He warned that another likely group who may be tempted to eat it were pregnant women, because they are known to lust after 'things most vile and filthy'.

I was told a similar story by a woman at one of my talks. She recounted how as a child of five she was a wedding reception in the local village hall. As a small child, she found the proceedings very, very boring, so she went outside to play in the sun. After a while she found a plant with lots of shiny black berries. She tasted one. It was sweet, so she ate several more before going back into the hall. Luckily her mouth and fingers were stained purple from the juice and she was rushed off to the local hospital where she was stomach pumped.

Deadly nightshade is sometimes known as *Dwale*, but there was a medicinal mixture that had the same name. It was used to send patients to sleep prior to a painful operation. The mixture included deadly nightshade and mandrake to help induce sleep. The other main ingredient was hellebore, which would help the body to quickly purge the poisons and reduce the risk of accidental death – if you had survived the operation! Most early herbals used deadly nightshade to send people to sleep, but it was considered very dangerous to use. Some people used the plant to intentionally send people to sleep forever. It was rumoured that Lucia Drusilla poisoned her husband, the Roman emperor, Augustus, by lacing some fresh figs with deadly nightshade.

The 'atropa' part of the botanical name refers to Atropos, one of the three *Morai*, or fates of classical mythology. Her younger sister Clotho spun the threads. The middle sister, Lachesis measured the length of the thread; the length of the life of a person. Atropos used her shears to cut the thread and end their life; making *Atropa* an appropriate name for such a poisonous plant.

The 'belladonna' part of the botanical name means 'beautiful lady'. The women of late medieval Italy, as fashion conscious then, as now, would take a preparation of deadly nightshade and drop it into their eyes to make their pupils dilate, which would make them more alluring to the men.

Atropine from belladonna is still used medicinally for the same purpose. The doctor will shine a light into the eye to make sure that the pupil can contract. Then atropine drops can be added to make the pupil expand so that the doctor can look into the interior of the eye to check for any damage. As the pupil dilates, there is a rush of light into the eye and the vision remains blurred for a few hours, so that the patient is not allowed to drive until normal vision returns. This has led me to wonder if the women put the belladonna into their eyes to make the men appear more attractive instead! Having received atropine during an eye examination, I rushed out

to the toilet to find a mirror so that I could look how my pupils had been affected. The black of the pupil had extended to the edge of the iris, and frankly, it looked weird, rather than beautiful.

Recent research has shown that men find women with enlarged pupils to be more attractive. Men were shown photographs of women, where some of the photos had been altered so that the pupils were enlarged. The men found the women with the larger pupils more alluring, but usually failed to notice the difference in the eyes. This may be one reason why a candlelit meal at a restaurant has a romantic feel to it. The dimmed lighting means that you tend to concentrate on your partner, but it also causes the woman's pupils to become enlarged.

Atropine eye drops were used in a case of murder in 2009, when a man's body was found in the boot of a car that had been left in a car park in France. The body had been cut in half across the stomach using a saw similar to the ones used in abattoirs. There was no blood on the cut edges of the body, so it was deduced that the body had been frozen before being cut in half. Tests were carried out with the result that atropine eye drops were found to be the cause of death.

It is rather surprising what people will admit to total strangers whom they think that they will never see again. I once met a woman at one of my historical gardening displays who told me that she had once added a small dose of deadly nightshade juice into some food; she then gave to her ex-husband, 'to teach him a lesson!' He was ill for several days as a result.

Just in case you find yourself with a potential poisoning from deadly nightshade, Berton Roueché wrote a short verse to help you to remember the effects of atropine poisoning;

'Mad as a hatter.
Blind as a bat.
Dry as a bone.
Red as a beet.
Hot as a pistol.'

DRAGONS

he name *Dracunculus* means little dragon, and the large purple spathe does resemble a dragon's head with a projecting tongue that is nearly black. The similarity becomes especially clear when the spathe begins to flop, as it usually does after three or four days, and become more horizontal than upright. The plant stem can grow to 1.5m tall; but you can add another 60cm for the spathe. It prefers shady position where the soil remains moist, but not water-logged.

Genus: *Dracunculis*
Species: *vulgaris*
Family: Araceae
Other Names:
   Dragons.
   Dragansia.
   Dragauns.
   Dragaces.
   Oderwourt.
   Serpentyn.
   Addyrwort.
   Neddretunge.
Herbaceous Perennial
Active Constituents:
   Oxalates of
   saponins.

You may have seen news reports of plants with a huge corm that can weigh about 50kg, and that produce a huge flower with a stench of rotting meat, *Amorphophallus titanum*, the Titan arum; *Dracunculus* is its smaller relative. Incidentally, the largest flower spike of a Titan arum, as recorded by the Guinness Book of Records, was grown by Louis Ricciardiello, of the USA, on 18 June 2010. It reached a height of 3.1m, making it a very large dragon.

If you fancy the thought of growing a giant arum, but can't afford to either buy or heat a huge greenhouse, then the little dragon is the plant for you. It is hardy and will happily grow outdoors in the garden. The smell is given off to attract flies for the pollination process. The first time that I grew the plant I had not known of its smelly reputation. I was weeding a flower bed at the foot of a barn wall. There was a smell of something dead. I thought that maybe a baby bird had fallen from a nest in the eaves. It took me some fifteen minutes to realise that it was the plant that was the source. The stench is at its worse during very hot weather. The stems are marked with blotches so that they resemble snakeskin, suggesting that the plant could be used to counter snake bites. So, if you were bitten by a European snake and made a concoction of the plant and drank it, the chances are such that you would survive. And if you did not take the medicine, the chances are also that you would survive, because unless you are very unfortunate, the chance of dying from the bite of most European snakes is quite low!

A slightly riskier recipe says that if a person rubs their hands with the root they will be able to handle adders without any risk. A side effect of trying this is the likelihood of the skin becoming red and peeling. The roots were used in the same manner as for cuckoo pint to remove freckles.

Dragons was used by the Physicians of Myddfai to cure cancer. The plants were cuts into small pieces, dried, and then crushed into a powder, which was boiled in wine. The patient should drink the liquid whilst it is warm, and continue to take the medicine for three days whilst fasting. They would then be cured and never have cancer again.

It was claimed that dragon roots drunk in wine stir up lechery, but it is not an aphrodisiac that I would wish to try in large doses, as it is even more powerful than cuckoo pint.

It was claimed that the dragon plant was a potent abortifacient;

> 'If a woman that is with child inhales the scent of the dragon flower when it withers it will deliver her of her werpling; and it will do the same if she places the root against her matrice.'

Although it is poisonous, the dragon is a plant well-worth growing in the garden, if for no other reason than the children will love the fact that it stinks.

FLY AGARIC

Fly agaric is the red capped toadstool with white flecks and a fairy sitting on top, that everybody knows from childhood books. The toadstool is the fruiting body which will release spores to start new colonies of fungi. The white spots are the remains of the covering of the toadstool head as it grows from the soil. Flay agaric has white gills underneath the cap and grows to 30cm tall and 20cm across in good conditions. It is

Genus: *Amanita*
Species: *muscaria*
Family: Amanitaceae
Other Names:
  Fly Agaric
Fungus
Active Constituents:
  Ibotenic acid.
  Muscarine.
  Muscimol.

usually found under birch and pine trees in woods and heathland. The mycelium of the fungus coats the tips of the roots of the tree that it lives beneath, which is beneficial to both, which is known as an ectomycorrizal relationship. The name fly agaric comes from its ancient use as a fly killer that has been recorded in many herbals. Pieces of the toadstool were placed in dishes of milk or water and left for the flies to take a sip - and then die.

During the 1970s, shamanic use of fly agaric started to become widespread. Some authors associated it with Christ, and others Santa Claus. One side effect of eating the fungus is that you lose the natural and useful, sense of fear. The Vikings had a group of soldiers, known as Berserkers, who would be the amongst the first to engage the enemy, charging in a wild frenzy, howling like animals, and completely fearless. They also chomped on their shields, as can be seen in some of the Lewis chess pieces. They wore different clothing to the rest of their companions, bear or wolf skins, so that they could be easily identified and avoided, because once in the berserk state, they fought whoever got in their way, friend and foe alike. It has been suggested that they ate the *Amanita muscaria* before going into battle. This use is not recorded in any Viking literature, but if this was the case, maybe it was considered a secret practice.

In some cultures, especially in Siberia, the toadstool would be eaten for its hallucinogenic effects; but not all of the constituents are metabolised and some are removed from the body in urine. The urine is saved and drunk when required and will have the same effects as the mushroom itself and according to some reports, without the nausea that comes from eating the toadstool flesh itself. The symptoms are of disassociation, distortion of vision and auditory hallucinations. There is little chance of dying from eating *Amanita muscaria*, because you will need to eat large amounts, which is unlikely to happen by accident as it is so distinctive. You are more likely to die as a result accidentally eating the destroying angel, *Amanita bisporigera*, or the death cap, *Amanita phalloides*, which responsible for many of the deaths from mushroom poisoning. The effects may not be noticed for several hours, or even days, by which time there will be irreversible kidney and liver damage. Half of a mushroom cap can cause death if not treated quickly enough. The typical symptoms are convulsions, delirium, diarrhoea and vomiting.

Whenever you forage for food from the countryside, be absolutely certain you have identified the plants correctly. Throughout most of history, people have been fearful of mushrooms for good reason.

FOXGLOVE

oxgloves are usually biennial plants. During the first year they produce a basal rosette of leaves, followed in the spring, by the tall flower spike that can reach a height of 2.5m. The flowers are purple, with white throats splashed with purple blotches. White flowered foxgloves are available, and if you want to grow only white foxgloves you must remove any purple ones before the plants can cross-pollinate. Sometimes the flower at the top of the flower spike becomes a *peloric* mutant. Usually the lower flower buds open first, but occasionally the flower at the tip

Genus: *Digitalis*
Species: *purpurea*
Family: Plantaginaceae
Other Names:
Foxgloves.
Our Lady's Gloves.
Fox's Thimbles.
Witch's Thimbles.
Biennial/Short-lived Perennial
Active Constituents:
Digoxin.
Digitoxin.
Gitoxin.

blooms first and the shape is like a large bowl, rather than the usual thimble bell. As a result, the flower spike will not be able to grow any taller.

Many people will say that it is too dangerous to grow monkshood in the garden, yet foxgloves are a common and much-loved garden plant. Most people know that they are poisonous, and all parts of the plant are poisonous; but they are not that concerned with the dangers of growing them. I spoke to a toxicologist who told me that on a toxicity scale of 1 to 20, where 1 is the most lethal, foxgloves are at number 3, the difference between a beneficial and a lethal dose being minute.

Foxgloves were certainly not a plant to be taken internally, unless under strict medical supervision. Gerard said that the ancients had no medical use for the plant, which is hardly surprising and Parkinson said that foxgloves were not used in medicine by any judicious man that he knew. The leaves look very similar to mullein or Aaron's Rod, a plant that has slightly furry silver leaves and tall stems bearing yellow flowers which was used internally as a medicine. This is a common mistake, but a more common case is that of people being unable to differentiate between the leaves of young foxgloves and those of Anchusa officinalis, a plant used to produce a red dye, which has small blue flowers.

William Withering is generally credited as being the first doctor to use foxgloves in the form of digitalis in modern medicine to help with heart disorders. He had originally learned of an herbal remedy for dropsy from an elderly woman in Shropshire, who was the local herbalist. Withering experimented with foxgloves for nine years; using different parts of the plant that had also been harvested at different times of the year to find the best way of producing a useful medicine. He recorded his experiments and published his discoveries in 1785 under the title of *An account of the foxglove and some of its medicinal uses: with practical remarks on dropsy, and other diseases.*

Erasmus Darwin had also used foxgloves for dropsy and had publicly announced this before Withering published his account, and the men fell out over the matter. Darwin may have published first, but Withering certainly carried out more practical research to ensure the safe and effective use of the drug.

GIANT HOGWEED

iant hogweed prefers to grow in moist soil. The leaves are often over 1m across. The stems are hollow and covered with red splashes. The leaves have irritant hairs growing from them. The flowers look very similar to a very large cow parsley. All parts of the plant are toxic. Giant hogweed was not mentioned in early herbals. The name is derived from Heracleon, which

Genus: *Heracleum*
Species: *mantegazzianum*
Family: Apiaceae
Common Name:
  Giant Hogweed.
Biennial
Active Constituents:
  Furocoumarin.

could possibly refer to Hercules, the super-hero of ancient myth.

Giant hogweed was introduced into Britain as a garden plant during the Victorian period. It was first recorded in England by the eminent garden writer, John Claudius Loudon, in 1836 in an article for the Gardeners Magazine. He wrote that he had it growing in his garden where it had reached a height of 12ft and that he intended to give seeds to his friends so they could also grow the plant, but that it had no practical use that he knew of. Loudon referred to the newly introduced plant as a Siberian Cow Parsnip.

The giant hogweed was grown for its large architectural leaves and the tall flower stems with white umbels of flowers that can produce up to 50,000 seeds that would rustle gently in the breeze.

In the older gardening books, there is no mention of the phototoxic burns on the skin that are produced in bright sunlight, that the plant is now mostly known for. As the writers of the time were intending their books to be read by the owners of the gardens, rather than the gardeners themselves, this may not be that surprising, and the gardeners were usually expected to remain fully covered and were often not even allowed to roll up their sleeves whilst working. The problems caused by the plant first became newsworthy in the 1970s when it was recorded that people had been affected by the plant, which was now becoming fairly common in the wilds as it spread along the banks of water courses, as the seed was carried downstream. I saw giant hogweed growing by a stream in Scotland during a visit in 1979. The leaves were so large that they smothered other plants completely, killing off all competitors for space, light, water and nutrients.

During the late summer of 2015, the plant made the news when several children wearing shorts and T shirts received serious burns after playing in a stand of giant hogweed on a bright sunny day. In 2013 a man nearly died as a result of trying to destroy the remains of the plant after having chopped it down. Sadly, the man was very badly injured by burns, but not those caused directly by contact with the plant; his injuries came from trying to start a fire using petrol! His employer mistakenly believed that giant hogweed could not be removed from a site for disposal, something that is true of Japanese knotweed, but not giant hogweed. It was decided to light a bonfire to burn the waste.

Because the plant is generally a biennial control is quite easy if you can prevent it seeding. The safest way to destroy a mature plant is to cut it down with a long handle slasher on a cloudy day, then let the remains dry out, when they will become inactive. Do not use a strimmer and do not chop the remains in a chipper.

HEDGE HYSSOP

Hedge Hyssop loves to grow in damp or wet areas, especially by ditches and other water courses, where it will grow out into the water. It grows to a height of 30cm and has a rhizomous root system and will spread quite rapidly in good growing conditions. The white flowers have purple markings and are trumpet shaped. All parts of hedge hyssop are poisonous and if taken internally it can cause bloody diarrhoea,

Genus: *Gratiola*
Species: *officinalis*
Family: Plantaginaceae
Other Names:
  Hedge Hyssop.
Herbaceous Perennial
Active Constituents:
  Gratiosid.
  Elaterinid.

vomiting, stomach ache, increased urine, which may then be followed by the inability, spasms, paralysis, and possibly death. I have never seen *Gratiola officinalis* growing in the wild, but it is fairly easy to buy from garden centres that sell aquatic plants. Culpepper said that this was one herb that was best left to an 'alchymist' to prepare as it was not otherwise safe to take internally. It was a violent purge, especially good for choler and phlegm, but also useful for dropsy, gout and sciatica. A cream could be made of it and rubbed onto the belly to remove intestinal worms, a much safer method than that proposed by some herbalists, who said it could be used internally for the same purpose.

Hedge hyssop was widely known to be an abortifacient, for which it would need to be taken in large doses, which would have made it a very dangerous process. A case was recorded where four women had been given a decoction of *Gratiola* as an enema, by some herb doctors. One of the women suffered violent vomiting and purging, and then became unconscious. He noted another surprising side-effect; that all the women had a strong attack of nymphomania. In another case a woman had constrictions of the throat and convulsions died two days after taking the medicine. Hedge hyssop is no longer used in general medical practice, but some homeopathic doctors still use it for gastral problems.

BLACK HELLEBORE

Black hellebore is named for its black roots rather than the flowers as is more usually the case for choosing a botanical name for a plant. The name 'helleborus' has been said to be from *helein*, meaning to cause death and, *bora*, meaning food, which is a good indicator that hellebores are poisonous.

The white flowers are often included on Christmas cards, as it is one of the few plants that are usually in flower over the Christmas period. The *orientalis* species tend to flower around Easter. Hellebore flowers are best shown to their advantage by cutting off the

Genus: *Helleborus*
Species: *niger*
Family: Ranunculaceae
Other Names:
  Christmas Rose.
  Hellebore.
  Clowetungge.
  Pedelyon.
  Ellebore.
  Lenten Rose - for the orientalis species.
Herbaceous Perennial
Active Constituents:
  Protoanemonin

leaves at ground level once the flowers have begun to open. The sap can cause blistering and the Royal Horticultural Society have recorded several cases of people developing rashes after putting hellebore leaves through a shredder before composting them.

In ancient Greece, there was a Temple of Apollo at Delphi, situated on the south west side of Mount Parnassus. The temple was considered to be at the centre of the world. One legend tells how Zeus wanting to find the centre of the earth, released two eagles flying at the same speed sending them in opposite directions. Their paths crossed above the site where Delphi now is. Zeus marked the point with a large stone known as the omphalos, or the navel of the earth. The temple had a high priest, the Pythia, who was an oracle, and when inspired by the god Apollo, she could foretell the future and offer advice and solutions to problems that were asked of her. The oracle could only be consulted on the seventh day of each month as this day was sacred to Apollo. A purification rite was carried out by the priestess to prepare herself before the applicants were allowed to ask their questions. The oracle would either inhale some fumes that issued from a cleft in the mountain, or according to other explanations, she would imbibe a sacred drink that included Laurus nobilis, the bay laurel. Her answer would be given in a form unintelligible to anybody but the priests, whom you would have to pay to interpret the answer for you and who often gave the answers in rhyming verses. Some of the answers were a bit ambiguous. One famous story told of a king who wanted to declare war on a local kingdom. He went to the Oracle of Delphi for her advice. He was told that if he went to war, a great kingdom would be destroyed. Feeling very optimistic, he duly went to war, and a great kingdom was destroyed; but it was his own kingdom. The temple and oracle attracted many pilgrims to Delphi. They generally sailed around the coast and landed at Corinth, from whence they would travel overland to reach the temple. Kirra was a strategically placed city on the pilgrim route that decided to take advantage of its position to rob pilgrims on their way to the temple. Other cities, possibly out of pique because they could not make money from the pilgrims, formed the Amphictionic League, to protect the rights of the temple at Delphi. The leaders of the League went to the oracle for advice and were told quite emphatically that they should declare war on Kirra. The League vowed to destroy Kirra and all of its inhabitants and also made a curse by the name of the god Apollo, that the soil would never be able grow crops again. War was duly declared and became known as the 'First Sacred War', but it went on for much longer than expected, lasting from 595 to 585 BCE. The leader of the League, Cleisthenes of Sicyon, blockaded the Gulf of Corinth with his navy, Kirra was then put under siege using the army. The city of Kirra seems to have stockpiled provisions and had a good source of water and offered no sign of surrender.

One version of what happened next was recounted by a Thessalos in the fifth century BC. One day, one of besiegers was riding his horse close to the city when the horse's hoof went into the ground, uncovering a hidden pipe that supplied Kirra with water, Nebros, a quick-thinking physician, noticed hellebores growing on the mountain side and had the brilliant idea of putting hellebores into the water supply, which would make the defenders ill and too weak to fight back when attacked. This is one of the earliest records of biological warfare. The plan was quickly carried out. The defenders, now suffering from diarrhoea, were quickly overcome and slaughtered and thus for once, the oracle was proved to be perfectly correct. So, if you receive a Christmas card with a pretty white flowered hellebore, remember that it has a rather grisly past associated with it.

The Agnus Castus herbal said that:

'The virtue of this herb is that the powder mixed with gruel or oatmeal will slay rats. Also, if a man or a beast pisse blood, give him this herb and he will assuredly be healed.'

The seeds have been used to poison rats and mice for centuries. Mascall wrote a book on how to make traps to catch various pests, and included several recipes to poison them too, including this one to kill mice:

'Take the powder of white Ellebore, otherwise called micing powder, and mire it with barley meale. Then put to honny, and make a paste thereof, then bake it, or leeth it, or frie it, and it will kill those mice that eates thereof.'

There were many other medicinal uses of hellebores; the finely ground root mixed with barley meal and used as plaster was said to dry up the humours of dropsy, or if used as a cosmetic it could clear spots and even cleanse lepers and remove all their scabs.

As with many other poisonous plants, it could also be used to stimulate the menses or bring out a dead child from the mother's womb. More improbable was its use to bring back the hearing of those who had gone deaf through sickness by being put in the ear for two or three days. Hellebore's main medicinal use was as a purge. Pliny said that a drachm of black hellebore would clean the stomach lightly, but he forbade giving more than four scruples at the most.

Coles said that hellebore was too dangerous to give to delicate people without correction, but that it was perfectly safe to give to country people as a simple, a medicine made of only one ingredient, because they had tougher bodies. He noted that it was the constitution of the patient and the quality of the medicine that should be taken into account when making a prescription; adding what is now a very common phrase, that, 'One man's meat, is another man's poison'.

Dr Salmon wrote that a brew of stinking hellebore, a native British plant, could be made to use as a vermifuge, to remove worms from the intestines, and that he had heard of several cases where stinking hellebore had killed people, adding, 'I am confident that if it does not kill the patient, it will certainly kill the worms'.

HEMLOCK

Hemlock grows to a height of 2.5m and prefers damp shady places, although it will happily grow in many other situations. It is one of the most common of the dangerous plants that may be found in the British countryside and has recently become more common in England as result of a series of wet summers. The plant has spread along the damp, shady hedgerows that provide ideal growing conditions. Hemlock is similar to many edible umbelliferous plants, (now reclassified as Apiaceae) plants that are used for human consumption, but it is fairly easy to identify with confidence in that it has red blotches on the stems that its edible relations do not have. All parts of the plant have what is often described as a 'mousey smell'.

Genus: *Conium*
Species: *maculatum*
Family: Apiaceae
Other Names:
  Hemlock.
  Spotted Hemlock.
  Poison Parsley.
Biennial
Active Constituents:
  Coniine.
  Methyl-coniine.
  Succus conii.

All parts of the plant are poisonous, although the roots are thought to be the least potent part. When the stems, leaves and seeds are dried the potency

of the plant is drastically reduced. In the past, the fresh, hollow stems have been used by children for making whistles or pea shooters. I have been told by people who have seen others suffer the effects that the lips and tongue of the victim will swell and burn, and if the tongue swells too much, it can become difficult to breath and swallow. Children no longer play with pea shooters very often, preferring computer games instead, so that is one problem that is going to become rarer in the future!

The remains of the medieval hospital at Soutra Aisle in Scotland have been excavated since 1986. When they were excavating, archaeologists discovered traces of a mixture of the seeds of hemlock, black henbane and opium poppy in one of the cellars. They believe the seeds may have been used as a general anaesthetic in the case of amputations, painful operations or perhaps even as a general painkiller in the way we would use ibuprofen. Another remedy, which monks may have found useful, was that a plaster of hemlock laid on the pubic area was said to quench lechery and the flow of semen.

In Shakespeare's play, *Hamlet*, Claudius decides to kill the elderly king Hamlet. If you wanted to kill a king at this period you would have had several options. Stabbing with sword or dagger would be messy and you would get covered in blood and quickly suspected. You could add poison to the king's food, but contrary to what historical novels suggest, many of the available poisons would be fairly slow acting, but show symptoms to arouse suspicion. Claudius was very clever. The elderly king was in the habit of going into his garden for a sleep under a tree on fine days. Claudius carefully poured his phial of poison into the king's ear as he slept. The poison was absorbed into the brain and everybody thought that the king had died peaceably in his sleep; at least until the ghost appeared…Some have suggested that hebanon, the poison that Shakespeare names, is hemlock, although others suggest it is yew.

The person most closely associated with hemlock is Socrates, a philosopher who lived during the fourth century BC. Socrates' philosophy was that you should think for yourself and not just do as you are told by your leaders. The rulers of Athens decided that this was not a good idea. Socrates was tried for treason and found guilty of corrupting the youth of Athens and sentenced to death. The Athenian method of inflicting the death penalty was for the convicted person to drink a goblet of hemlock juice. If using fresh hemlock, you simply mash the stems with a pestle and mortar, a kitchen whizzer would do equally well today, and strain the juice into the goblet. Socrates accepted the verdict and prepared himself for his fate. He was surrounded by his friends and after making a sacrifice to the gods he drank the hemlock. Socrates had asked for a physician to be present and described the effects of the poison. The poison acts slowly by causing paralysis of the central nervous system. You lose the sense of feeling from the extremities, the fingers and toes, which gradually works towards the heart. Death can take an hour or so.

Another macabre use of hemlock was that when the inhabitants of the island of Cea reached the age of sixty or above, and became unable to be of further use to their community, they would voluntarily take hemlock so as not to become a burden to the others.

Rufinus wrote in his herbal of two boys who lived in Ravenna who had agreed to a gamble; the loser of the bet was to take a dose of lethal hemlock. The matter on which they were gambling on is not recorded, but the bet took place, and the loser was found dead the following day. It is not known whether the loser was aware that one antidote for hemlock was to drink hot wine. As with many antidotes given in the early herbals, it was unlikely to work, but if he had drunk enough wine, it would have at least taken his mind of his impending fate.

Coles includes the rather gruesome information, that when asses had eaten hemlock they often fell into such a deep sleep that their owners had thought they had died, and so, they flayed the asses for their skins, but:

> 'later, when the effects of the hemlock had worn off and the poor animals awaked much to their own distress and the grief and amazement of their owners… and to the laughter of others.'

Shakespeare's witches certainly made use of the plant, as they went to collect 'root of hemlock digg'd in the dark'. There may be several reasons for digging the root in the dark, the obvious one being to avoid detection when harvesting a poisonous root. Another is that plants for herbal remedies were often collected at times when it was believed they would be at their most potent. The cycles of the moon were thought to affect the growth of plants, so the times for sowing and the harvesting of plants were synchronised to the phases of the moon. It had been noticed that a full moon caused higher tides. It was thought that plants were influenced in a similar way. If you required leaf growth for crops such as cabbage, lettuce and spinach you would sow and harvest your crops at a waxing or full moon when the moon was drawing water from the soil into the leaves. If you were growing root vegetables you would sow and harvest on a waning moon or a dark moon, the moisture thereby remaining in the roots. Shakespeare's witches were not only hidden from view, but the hemlock root was being dug up when it was at its best.

Because of the sedative, anti-spasmodic and paralysing effects of coniine, it has been used to counter-act the violent muscles contractions of strychnine poisoning. For the thriftily minded, hemlock seeds have been used to poison rats, mice and birds; at no cost to the gardener.

HEMP

Cannabis is one plant that many people know from the shape of the leaf, even if they have never seen the plant in real life. There are two main sub species, *Cannabis sativa* subsp. *sativa* and *Cannabis sativa* subsp. *indica*, and after that it can become very confused. The *Cannabaceae* family has another well-known member, hops, which are also said to have a soporific effect.

Genus: *Cannabis*
Species: *sativa*
Family: Cannabaceae
Common Names:
  Cannabis.
  Marijuana.
  Pot.
  Weed.
  Skunk.
  Ganja.
Annual
Active Constituents:
  Tetrahydrocannabinol
  (THC)

Hemp has been grown in England since the medieval period to produce strong fibres. It was mostly grown in the Fenland around Holland and Ely but also other places, such as Suffolk. In 1557, Thomas Tusser wrote a book in rhyming couplets, *A Hundred Points of Good Husbandry*, later extended to, *Five Hundred Points of Good Husbandry*, to assist famers in planning their working year. He included a verse for July, showing some of the uses of hemp:

'Wife, pluck fro thy seed hemp, the fimble hemp clean,
This looketh more yellow, the other more green:
Use t'one for thy spinning, leave Michell the t'other,
For shoe-thread and halter, for rope and such other.'

The diarist Samuel Pepys recorded an unpleasant journey through the Fens, noting that on 17 September 1663:

'... I begun a journy with them; and with much ado through the Fens, along Dikes, where sometimes we were ready to have our horses sink to the belly, we got by night, with great deal of stir and hard riding, to Parsons drove, a heathen place - where I found my uncle and aunt Perkins, and their daughters, poor wretches, in a sad poor thatched cottage, like a poor barne or stable, peeling of Hemp (in which I did give myself good content to see their manner of preparing of hemp) and in a poor condition of habitt; took them to our miserable Inne and there, after long stay and hearing of Franke their son, the miller, play upon his Treble (as he calls it), with which he earnes part of his living, and singing of a country bawdy song, we set down to supper: the whole Crew and Frankes wife and children (a sad company, of which I was ashamed) supped with us.'

Daniel Defoe travelled extensively throughout Britain and recorded his experiences in his book, *Tour thro' the whole Island of Great Britain*, published between 1724 to 1726. Concerning his journey through the Fenland regions he noted that hemp was still a major crop in the region:

> 'Here are the greatest improvements by planting of hemp, that, I think, is to be seen in England; particularly on the Norfolk and Cambridge side of the Fens, as about Wisbech, Well, and several other places, where we saw many hundred acres of ground bearing great crops of hemp.'

An article in the *Annals of Agriculture and Other Useful Arts*, dated 23 June 1788, by an anonymous author, discussed hemp production in Suffolk including the various methods of production and processing of the hemp. It was an economically viable crop as the average harvest was 36 to 38 stone of hemp per acre, but in a good year it could be as much as 60 stone per acre. The hemp was dried and stacked over the winter, and in January or February, especially if snow had fallen, the dried plant material is spread over the meadows to be retted, so that the covering on the stems would start to rot so the fibres could be extracted. This method gave an inferior quality fibre, suitable for coarse cloth, compared to water retting, where the hemp was tied in small bundles and stood in water for four to six days. When you were able to rub the bark off by hand, the bundles were spread out on the meadows. Later the stems were beaten using a device called a brake. Some of the smaller fibres would break and these were bundled separately and sold as shorts, at half the price of the best fibres which were called longs. These were tied in bundles, each weighing a stone; a stone in Suffolk being 14.5 pounds at that time. The dew-retted hemp sold at 1 shilling, sometimes as much as 2 shilling per stone, whilst the best water retted hemp sold for considerable more, from 8 shillings and six pence. The hemp was sold to the hicklers, who beat the hemp to separate the fibres, after which it was combed. The hicklers earned 3 farthings to 2d. per pound, giving them a rate of pay from 15d. to 2 shillings a day. The fibres were graded according to the needs of the spinners, who spun the fibres into threads, which they sold to the weavers. A journeyman weaver could earn 1s. to 21s.6d. per day. The best woven hemp was used for tablecloths and towels. The lesser hemp was used to make clothing for servants, husbandmen and labouring manufacturers. Better quality hemp, selling at 18d. to 2s. a yard, was worn by farmers and tradesmen. The finest hemp cloth sold at 2s.6d. to 3s.6d. per yard, and was preferred by gentleman as it was warmer and stronger than other linen cloths.

The crop continued to be grown during the Victorian period, and it is recorded that many of the workers who handled the hemp plants complained that it made them feel ill, giving them headaches and nausea.

Hemp is still used to make clothing and items such as bags and purses, but the hemp plant now grown for the fibres does not contain the toxic substances, THC, that produce the effects so beloved by recreational drug users. As a commercial plant, hemp is ideal as it suffers from few pests or diseases and does not need fertiliser. This cultivar is grown legally in many countries, but it is not legal to grow it in the UK as the government is concerned that it may become a front for growing the illegal species. Hemp seed is useful for fishermen, who cook the seeds and attach it to the hook as a bait or throw it into the water to attract more fish to their hooks. Some web sites suggest using as much as one to two kg of seeds in well stocked, still waters to attract fish to your position. Hemp seed is sold in many health food shops because it contains omega 3 and omega 6 oils, gamma-linolenic acid (GLA)) and fairly high concentrations of vitamin E, so the hulled seeds are often used to make snack bars. Cold pressed hemp oil is used for cooking oil, salad dressings, as a food supplement taken in capsules and for cosmetics, such as shampoos, soaps and lip balms.

Hemp seed was once an ingredient in the commercially available Swoop bird food, that people bought to put on bird tables. It was common knowledge that the mix often contained cannabis seeds and there are many reports of cannabis plants having grown from fallen seed, or seed that had been planted on purpose. One case involved the police themselves, when cannabis plants were found to be growing at the Thorpe Wood police station in Peterborough! Due to the threat to bio-security, most seeds for bird food that are not native to Britain are treated to make sure they will not grow and become a problem by escaping into the wild.

During the Victorian period and the early 1900s, cannabis was grown as a garden plant. It was often recommended for the back of the border because although the flowers are not particularly attractive, the plant has good foliage to act as a backdrop for the more decorative plants. The *Gardeners' Assistant* of 1878 described cannabis as a strong growing annual suitable for planting in groups or singly. Growing from ten to fifteen feet high, with palmate leaves, it was considered too coarse for the best flower beds close to the main lawn, but it was suitable for the shrubbery borders or as a background for finer flowering or foliage plants. Erasmus Darwin, grandfather to Charles Darwin, mentioned a new species of hemp that was grown by K. Fitzgerald Esq, which was thought to be superior to other species that had been grown in England until that point in time. The seeds were sown on 4 June and grew to a height of fourteen feet seven inches with a girth of seven inches by the middle of October. The plant was said to have grown seven inches in a week when the weather was good.

Growing cannabis is, of course, illegal in Britain, but there is a false hemp plant, *Datisca cannabina*, that has a passing similarity to the real cannabis plant, but if you do grow it, just hope that nobody steals it in mistake for the real thing.

As a recreational drug, cannabis has acquired many names; most of which were taken from the way that the plant was prepared or used. *Hashish*, or *Hasheesh* is the resin that oozes from the leaves, stems and tops of the female plants. In some production areas, men wearing leather overalls would run through the standing plants, so the resin would stick to the leather and could then be scraped off. In other places, the leaves were rubbed between two carpets so the resin stuck to the carpet fibres and then be scraped off. It is usually smoked, often through water pipes, such as hookah pipes.

Bhang is the dried larger leaves of the plant added to other things such fruits, sugar and water and usually taken as a drink. It is one of the ingredients used to make a sweet called *majun* or *majoun*, which is made with nuts, honey, dried fruits, and of course, cannabis. The ingredients are mixed together and rolled into small balls. *Ganja* is the dried tops of the female plants and smoked to inhale the fumes.

There are now other processes, to which can be added THC-rich resins: hash oil; wax, a soft solid; and shatter, containing about 80 per cent THC, which is made into a hard lump like glass and will shatter if hit.

One story is that the name hashish derives from the suicide sect, the Assassins. The sect developed during the crusades as western Europeans tried to recapture Jerusalem from the Muslims. The assassins' mission, much the same as today's suicide bombers, was to attack leaders and prominent members of the crusaders. How do you make the would-be assassins fearless with no sense of personal mortality in the face of certain death? According to one Islamic tradition a man receives the services of seventy-two virgins when he reaches paradise. The story is that the young male recruits would be doped on hashish and then taken to a garden where they would waken to find many young girls tending to them; they think they are in paradise. They would then be doped again and taken back to the original place once more. On reawakening, they believed that they had received a vision of paradise and became fearless. Another explanation of the name is that the assassins took the drug to make themselves fearless. One wonders if this is still one method to make modern suicide bombers equally fearless.

Culpepper simply called the plant hemp. It must have been a common sight as he did not even bother to describe it because he said that everyone knew what it looked like. He recommended the seed for wind, but warned, as did Dioscorides and others since then, that too much could dry up the semen.

If a patient suffered from internal bleeding of the mouth, nose and other places, you could fry the leaves with the blood of the patient. The root was used for gout and the general aches and pains of the joints, as many of those who suffer from multiple sclerosis have since discovered.

Today cannabis plants attract the headlines of the local press when a rented house is discovered to have been stripped out inside and been converted to make a 'cannabis farm' by growing the plants using a hydroponic system. Quite a few of the farms have been detected by police helicopters using infra-red detectors as the houses are much hotter than the ones around them and are easily spotted. Many cases are recorded by the local and national press. One of the most interesting cases was reported in February 2017, when a nuclear shelter dating from the 1980s was raided after people locally reported the smell coming from the bunker vents. A crop of cannabis plants was discovered growing in the twenty rooms with a potential street value of £1m. Cannabis farms are illegal, but there is the associated problem of human trafficking and the modern slave trade. Many of the workers in the illegal farms are often illegal immigrants of Vietnamese origin with no documents, who are of an uncertain age and are kept confined within the farms in very inhumane conditions.

At one garden where I worked, the person who lived there had grown some cannabis plants in the greenhouse. He asked me to plant them in the garden. I pointed out that a regular visitor was a policeman who trained the local forces dogs and often called in for a cup of tea when the garden was open. I was told to hide the plants behind some large tomato plants that I had trained up tall canes. For good measure, I roped off the area so people would not get close enough to notice the cannabis plants.

HENBANE

Henbane is an attractive plant with hairy leaves that have a peculiar scent. The flowers are a buff colour with attractive dark purple markings. The stamens are a very bright violet until pollination has taken place. The whole plant is poisonous. The plant is mostly an annual but can be biennial too by removing the flowering stems before seed can form. Any plant that is named as a bane is usually poisonous; in this case as the name suggests, it was thought to be notably poisonous for

Genus: *Hyoscyamus*
Species: *niger*
Family: Solanaceae
Common Names:
 Henbane.
 Hog's Bean.
 Jupiter's Bean.
Annual/Biennial
Active Constituents:
 Atropine.
 Scopolamine.
 Hyoscyamine.

poultry, although it is lethal to many other species too.

Henbane is probably not a true native plant and may have been introduced by the Romans. Old books say that it grew on rubbish piles, waste land and sandy beaches. Brook called henbane:

'a poisonous and dangerous plant, of a dismal aspect and disagreeable smell. The farm-yards and ditch banks in most places are full of it.'

Rubbish piles are less common now, and so is the plant. The only time I have ever seen henbane growing wild was on Lindisfarne Island, Northumbria.

John Arderne warned how the rogues of France used a potion to send fellow travellers, especially pilgrims, to sleep against their will so that they could then rob them of their silver:

'The seeds of henbane, darnel, black poppy, white bryony and crush them to a fine powder in a brass mortar. The powder can be added to the victim's pottage, cake or drink, after which he may sleep all day.'

Travellers in India risked similar treatment from thieves, but the plant of preference there was *Datura stramonium*.

Henbane contains a relatively high concentration of tropane alkaloids primarily atropine, hyoscyamine and scopolamine. Scopolamine is mostly responsible for the effects of intoxication followed by narcosis, leaving the victim in the transitional state between consciousness and sleep. Witches are alleged to have used it in their flying ointments. In a television documentary, *Sacred Weeds*, people took several plant-based drugs, all perfectly legally, whilst under medical supervision. One of the plants that featured in the series was henbane, and although the dosage was very low, one of the volunteers who took the henbane described how he felt as if he was flying.

In his book of 1584, *Discoverie of Witchcraft*, Reginald Scott gave two recipes for making flying ointments, but Henbane is not included in either example.

'Some receipts and ointments made and used fore the transportation of witches.

'The fat of young children, and seeth it with water in a brazen vessel, reserving the thickest of that which remaineth boiled in the bottome, which they laie up and keeps, until occasion serveth to use it. They put hereunto Eleoselinum, Aconitum, Frondes populeas, and soote.'

Another recipe to the same purpose.

'Sium, Acarum vulgare, pentaphyllon, the blood of a flitter-mouse, solanum somniferum, & oleum. They tempe all these together, and then they rubbe all parts of their bodies exceedinglie, till they look red, and verie hot, so as thoer pores may be opened, and their flesh soluble and loose. They joine here withal either fat, or oile insteed thereof, that the force of the ointment maie the rather pearse inwardly, and so be more effectually. By this meanes, (saith he) in a moone light night they seeme to be carried in the aire, to feasting, singing, dancing, kissing, culling, and other actes of venerie, with such youths as they love and desire most: for the force (saith he) of their imagination is so vehement, that almost all part of the braine, wherein the memory consistith is full of such conceipts. And whereas they are naturallie prone to believe anie thing; so doo they receive such impressions and steadfast imaginations into their minds, as even their spirits are altered thereby: not thinking upon anie thing else, either by daie or by night.'

In this recipe, it is the *Solanum somniferum*, deadly nightshade, that produces the magic.

Coles said that the ointment was reported to use the fat of babies dug out of their graves and that some thought the most likely drugs to use for the flying affect would come from not only henbane, but hemlock, mandrake, nightshade, tobacco, opium, saffron, opium and poplar leaves.

Besides being rubbed vigorously onto the body, the mix could possibly have been applied to the broomstick, and the witch would then straddle her broom. In those days women did not wear underwear, so the toxic mix would soon be absorbed into the blood stream and the witch would think that she was flying. The later inquisitors were quite explicit that the witch fell asleep after using the ointment and described their flying journey only when they woke up.

One herbal warned that:

'This herb and its seeds do much good in medicines. But if it is eaten as wortys, it will bring the eaters into a state into the type madness known as manya (mania). And also the juice will do the same if it is held to a wound, wherever it may be.'

In Shakespeare's play *Macbeth*, Banquo called henbane the insane root due to its effects on the mind:

'Or have we eaten of the Insane Root
That takes reason prisoner?'

But henbane had many other uses. For a woman whose breasts ached, a drink of the juice would cure her, but it may have led to unforeseen consequences. The powdered leaves could be mixed with flour and used as a poultice on boils, or if you needed to slay any worms in the ears, you could pour henbane juice into the ear to kill them or to cure any other pains in the ear.

Grind the seed to a powder and make a paste with wine and apply to the testicles to cure boils, but there was a warning that if the juice got into an open wound will become wooden as if in a mania.

Gerard spoke of a common ploy used by the travelling doctors who claimed to be able to cure tooth ache. Under the Doctrine of Signatures, the stem of henbane with the developed seed cases along it, had the appearance of a jaw bone and teeth. It was once believed that toothache was caused by a worm that was wriggling at the base of the tooth. If you have ever had toothache, it is easy to understand why. The travelling quack doctor would place some burning charcoal in a dish and place some henbane seeds over and allow them to begin to burn. The patient was asked to inhale the smoke thorough their mouth, allegedly to kill the worms causing the toothache. The henbane seed smoke would act as a painkiller and the tooth would cease to hurt. Then to prove that the worms were in fact dead, the doctor would ask the patient to open their mouth over a bowl of water- and Voila! The worms could be seen wriggling in the water! But Gerard then reveals that the worms were in fact short pieces of lute strings. The lute strings, being made of catgut, would move about as they began to absorb water. The patient would be allowed to see the worms, before the bowl was quickly removed before the truth could be discerned. I have used this as part of historical herbalist demonstration, and it works very well.

Henbane could be used to induce sleep. The Physicians of Myddfai mixed henbane and eryngo seeds and pounded them in a mortar and mixed the powder with milk to make pills. The dose was one pill every half hour, and after six or eight pills the patient would be asleep. A similar recipe used the juice of opium poppies, in which case the dose was a pill every two to three hours, with the proviso that you observe the effect on the patient before giving them another pill.

I once met a man who told me that he regularly steeped the seeds of henbane in a bottle of wine for a few days before drinking the wine. From his physical and mental state, this is definitely not something that I could recommend trying.

The most notorious murder case involving henbane is that of Dr Hawley

Harvey Crippen, who was born in Michigan in 1862. He had qualified as a homeopathic doctor at the Cleveland Homeopathic Hospital in 1885, but he did not have the correct qualifications to be entitled to being designated a doctor in England, although he was still referred to as Dr Crippen during his trial. During his trial, Crippen said that he had been married before in New York to a lady named Bell, who had died in either 1890 or 1891. In 1893, he met Cora Turner, as she called herself. Her real name was Clara Mackamotski, aged 17, and she was living under the protection of a man named Lincoln. Crippen and Clara eloped and lived in St Louis before they were later married.

Crippen moved to England in April 1897 and Cora followed him in August. Initially their apartments were in South Crescent, just off Tottenham Court Road, where they lived for about a year. After several house moves, they eventually settled at Hilldrop Crescent in 1905. Crippen had to visit America, and it was during his time away that Cora, who was working as a Music Hall entertainer, using the stage name of Belle Elmore, met Bruce Miller, described during the later trial as 'a member of the music hall profession', who sent her letters of an amorous tone and often signed off with 'Love and kisses to Brown Eyes'.

During Crippen's trial, Miller claimed that he had not had an affair with Cora, stating that it was a platonic relationship, as they were both already married – but he seems to have only visited Cora when her husband was not at home.

On his return to England Crippen noticed a change in his wife, who constantly criticised him; he may have seen some of the letters from Miller. Cora admitted to him that she had met somebody else and Crippen later claimed she threatened to leave him for her new admirer. Crippen began an affair with Ethel le Neve, the proverbial younger woman, but who was also his secretary or 'the typist', as Cora referred to her. Crippen thought that Cora was unaware of his affair, and he had told Ethel that he would marry her when Cora was no longer around. From the law's point of view that was certainly a motive for murder. Crippen said that Cora provoked an argument at home when they had invited Mr and Mrs. Martinetti to dinner. According to Crippen, Cora had once more threatened to leave him, and he did not see her again. Crippen's neighbours began to be concerned for her safety and informed the police that they had not seen her for some time. The police spoke to Crippen at his house, where he told them that he had received a letter from Cora to say that she had met somebody else and gone back to America; however, he had burned the letter. Satisfied with his explanation, the police went away. Crippen was uncertain whether the police believed him or not, so he and Ethel le Neve fled to Antwerp and boarded the SS *Montrose*, which was bound for Quebec. Captain Kendall, the master of the SS *Montrose*, became suspicious of two of his passengers, a Mr John Robinson and a Master Robinson, his 16-year old son, and used the new wireless telegraph system to alert his ship owners of his suspicion that they were in reality Crippen and Ethel le Neve.

During one of my talks, a man told me that when he was a boy, he had been told that Captain Kendall became suspicious when he threw a ball for Master Robinson to catch. Rather than remaining standing to catch the ball, as any young man would normally do, Master Robinson squatted down as if he was more used to catching a ball by squatting down; as if being more used to wearing a skirt or dress than trousers.

Whatever aroused his suspicions, the captain sent the message to say that he suspected he had Crippen on board. Inspector Walter Dew caught a faster ship across the Atlantic. He landed and boarded a pilot craft which steamed out to meet the SS *Montrose* before Crippen could land. This was the first example of a ship-to-shore telegraph being used to catch a fugitive murderer. A verse of the time recorded the event:

'Dr Crippen killed Belle Elmore
Ran away with Miss le Neve
Right across the ocean blue
Followed by Inspector Dew
Ship's ahoy, naughty boy!'

Meanwhile the police had become suspicious once more, and returned to the house for further investigation. As police still do today, they began to dig under the brick floor in the cellar. They found the remains of a body. There were no bones, not even the skull; just a folded parcel of skin. Crippen had often changed his story of what had happened, which did not inspire confidence in his version of events. Hyoscine, made from henbane, was discovered in the internal organs of the body, and as a physiological test, some of the extract was dropped into one eye of a cat and both eyes were then exposed to a bright light. The pupil with the added hyoscine became dilated, proving the presence of hyoscine in the body.

Later examination of the folded skin seemed to suggest there was a scar on the belly and such a scar on Cora's belly was confirmed by Crippen himself. The counsel for the defence said that there were hairs growing in the alleged scar, proving that it was not a scar, because hair cannot grow in scar tissue, but the claim failed to save Crippen's life. The trial lasted a week. He was found guilty and hanged on 23 November 1910 at HMP Pentonville, London. Ethel le Neve was tried, found not guilty and acquitted. Crippen had certainly bought quantities of hyoscine before Cora disappeared. He claimed to be using it for medicines that he was making for various treatments to treat such conditions as nervous disorders. He said that he remembered buying the drug on 19 January and that he made up preparations using two thirds of it; and described how he had prepared it, but he was unable to remember who the patients were as there were so many of them. Neighbours and friends testified that Hawley and Cora Crippen appeared to be on good terms and acted civilly towards each other, and Crippen himself was described as being of a good temper. Recently some have suggested that the body was not Cora Crippen and the DNA test of the body suggest that it may have even been a man.

The male DNA results could be explained by contamination of the remains by the unprotected investigating policemen, who had no idea about the future discovery of DNA, and that their primitive methods could possibly have such long-term or far-reaching effects. Also, the woman that was claimed to be a descendant of Cora Crippen seems to have no birth certificate to prove her lineage. But if Cora Crippen was still alive, what happened to her and where did she go? One thing is certain, if Cora was still alive, she did not come forward to save her husband. For me, the verdict is still unclear. If Crippen had successfully disposed of the bones and skull, why not the innards and skin; especially the skin with the scar? People will continue to argue about the evidence. Some to prove that Crippen was guilty; others to show his innocence. But like all great mysteries, we may never know for certain.

HOLLY

olly is one of the few trees that just about everybody can recognise, if only because of Christmas. Holly grows to about 25m, but is usually shorter than that in most gardens. The flowers are a greenish white and have four petals, followed by red berries that can still be found on many trees even during the summer. It is the berries that are toxic, causing diarrhoea, stomach pain, and vomiting. The tree is usually male or female, which has led to some confusing

Genus: *Ilex*
Species: *aquifolium*
Family: Aquifoliaceae
Other Names:
   Holly.
   Christ's Thorn.
Evergreen Tree
Active Constituents:
   Ilicine.
   Tannine.
   Theobromine.

cultivar names. 'Silver Queen', a holly with white variegated edges on the leaves and 'Golden Queen' with yellow variegations on the leaves are both actually male plants and will not bear berries; likewise, 'Golden King' is a female holly and has bright red berries that look very attractive set against the yellow and green leaves. I have mixed feelings about growing holly in my own garden as the leaves turn up all over the place and cause unexpected pain as I am weeding.

In a garden setting, holly has been used for hedging and topiary for centuries. The gentleman gardener, Thomas Hanmer, said that holly could be cut into any shape, especially as it had beautiful leaves and berries. He remembered seeing an avenue of holly cut into tall pyramids that were well clothed with leaves from the ground to the tops. One observation that Hanmer made, that is still relevant today, is that holly dislikes being transplanted. At one garden where I worked we lost dozens of rather large, and expensive, hollies that were container-grown. The smaller ones survived.

Holly has many folklore associations. Christianity used all parts of the tree, as the well-known carol, *The Holly and the Ivy*, illustrates. The white flowers symbolise purity and became linked to Mary, the leaves represent the crown of thorns and the red berries are the drops of Christ's blood. The bark is very bitter, the bitterness and sadness of existence from which Christ will save us. In the battle of the sexes the holly is male; tall, proud and erect. The ivy is female, she cannot stand alone and needs the male to support her; hence the Holly bears the crown. The old carol, *The Contest of the Ivy and the Holly*, has the refrain:

'Nay, ivy, nay, it shall not be I wis;
Let holly have the mastery, as the manner is.'

A sentiment that today would be considered as very politically incorrect indeed. Parkinson wrote that:

'The branches with berries, are used at Christ tide to decke our houses withal, but that they should defend the house from lightning, and keepe themselves from witchcraft, is a superstition of the Gentiles, learned from Pliny, saith Matthiolus.'

The bark had a more practical use as an ingredient for making birdlime as it would be easier to find holly bark, rather than to use mistletoe berries that were said to make the best birdlime. Gerard described the process used by the country men, who took holly branches and stripped off the bark. Then they made a ditch in moist and boggy soil and filled it with the holly bark and covered it over with other boughs. The bark was left for about twelve days by which time it would be rotten and putrefied. The bark was then beaten in mortars until it was thick and clammy, when it was washed to remove any remaining pieces of bark and waste. When it was clean, nut oil was added and mixed together to make the birdlime, which was then stored in earthenware jars for later use. The thick lime was like a glue and was smeared onto branches to catch small birds. Gerard advised that the birdlime should not be used as medicine as it would glue up all of the patient's entrails and could be fatal. But he was happy to suggest the use of the untreated berries as a medicine;

> 'Ten or twelve berries would remove the thick phlegmatic humours by the stool, as those who have tried it have verified. and the bark crushed to a powder were both good for the stomach, dispersing the wind, dysentery and other fluxes.'

The wood is very hard and a thin sapling can be used to make a sturdy walking stick. A knobkerry is a walking stick, but was also used as a weapon to give an opponent a good blow to the head. They were made from a sapling with a large rounded root, usually of blackthorn, but holly was also used.

Holly leaves are still used by modern herbalists as an astringent, a mild diuretic, and to help influenza, bronchitis and pneumonia. The berries are no longer used as they are too dangerous.

HORSE TAIL

The genus name comes from the Latin *equus*, for a horse and *seta*, a bristle. Equisetum prefers a moist soil and has been used as an indicator of an underground source of running water. It has thin, black, rhizome roots that are difficult to remove completely, so the plant can quickly spread if you leave any part of the root in the soil or in the footings of walls or under the path. It is not a weed that you would want in your garden. Miller commented that they were:

Genus: *Equisetum*
Species: *arvense*
Family: Equisetaceae
Common Names:
  Horse Tail.
  Bottle Brush.
  Shave Grass.
  Pewter Wort.
  Dutch Rushes
Herbaceous Perennial
Active Constituents:
  Aconitic acid.
  Saponins.
  Silicic compounds.

'… found in England, on the sides of ditches, or in shady woods; but as they are plants which are never cultivated in gardens, I shall pass them over in this place.'

And most of us would agree with him, because the plant is very invasive and virtually impossible to eradicate, although some garden centres now sell equisetum for planting with water features. If you do have equisetum growing as a weed in your garden, you will discover that the high content of silica in the leaves, and stems, especially in the epidermis, help them to resist chemical weed killers. The recommended application method is to hit the stems with a stick to bruise them, and then apply the weed killer.

The plant produces two types of stem. The white fertile stems are hollow, and appear in the spring, growing to 25cm tall. They have a rather phallic-looking spore cone at the tip which is a brownish colour. The green sterile stems begin to grow as the fertile stems start to wilt, growing to just under 1m. tall and have hollow, vertically grooved segments with whorls of side shoots that resemble a chimney sweeps brush. Each individual segment can be pulled apart from its neighbour. The equisetums date back to the time of the dinosaurs, an indication of just how tough they are. The Oxford Museum at Woodstock recently created a display of a *Tyrannosaurus rex* surrounded by a tall species of equisetum. This area is set apart from the rest of the garden, reducing the risk of the equisetum spreading to other parts of the garden.

Hildegard said that mare's tail grew from the bad humours of the earth and that it offered no benefits to anybody who ate it; but if you could add it to bait for flies, they would be killed by the bad humours that it possessed.

When there were many pewter workshops in Birmingham, there were fields of equisetum which was harvested and burned. The ashes were used to polish the pewter. I have used fresh and dried stems to demonstrate how effective they are for cleaning rusty iron. Many re-enactors use horsetail for cleaning pots and pans, which is another traditional use. I have met several older people who have told me that when they were younger some of the villagers used the plant in the same way. Gerard said that housewives used it to scour their pewter and wooden kitchen utensils; whilst Fletchers and Comb makers used it to 'rub and polish their work'. In Northumbria, if not elsewhere, it was used by dairy maids to scour and clean their milk pails. I have found it good for polishing glass. The plant was imported from Holland, leading it to acquire another name, Dutch Rushes, although this seems to have been Equisetum hyemale as it is much coarser than E. arvense. It was used by whitesmiths and cabinet makers. The plant was so rough that it was said that if cows ate it their teeth would drop out, but Brook said that he could not say if this was true, but the pasture must be very bad for the cows to be compelled to eat it.

Musicians also used horsetail; hurdy gurdy players used it to clean the wheel of their instrument because when there is too much resin on the surface it may become uneven, and make the notes sound 'lumpy'.

Medicinally equisetum was known as *Cauda Equina*. Dioscorides said that it had binding and cooling properties and good for healing wounds. Most later herbalists agreed that it was good for wounds, nose bleed, the bloody flux and to reduce menstrual bleeding. It has a traditional use for strengthening brittle finger and toe nails and brittle bones and Brook noted that it had once been used as a cure for gonorrhoea, but that it was out of the present practice.

It is now recommended that the plant is only internally used for short periods. Although generally considered safe, it may cause nausea, diarrhoea, excess urination, visual problems and low levels of vitamin B1.

Horsetail used on the hair is said to reduce dandruff and help the hair to grow. Wash your hair with shampoo, then rinse through with a brew made of horsetail and leave it for about ten minutes as if using a conditioner, then rinse it out.

IVY

I vy is the most common of the UK's native evergreen plants. It is very useful in the garden as it forms a thick mat to provide excellent ground cover. It can be trained to grow up walls and trellis to shield unsightly views and variegated cultivars can add colour to a dark position. Personally, I would never allow ivy to grow on drystone walls as the roots will thicken inside the wall and eventually split it open; I prefer not to have ivy growing on brick walls either, as the suckers can remain on

Genus: *Hedera*
Species: *helix*
Family: Araliaceae
Common Names:
 Ivy.
 Tree Ivy.
Evergreen Climber
Active Constituents:
 Triterpenoid
 saponins.
 Falcarinol.

the wall for some time after you remove the ivy. They are very difficult to remove except with a stiff wire brush or a scraper.

English Heritage produced a document that said that ivy would hold old walls together and prevent them falling over; which is true to some extent, until you want to remove the ivy, when you may find that the wall is beyond repair and must be dismantled and rebuilt. Ivy growing in trees will eventually kill off branches as it smothers them and eventually makes the trees liable to being damaged or blown over by strong winds. Ivy stems have small growths that look a little like roots that have small discs on the end, and it is these that can adapt to cling to stone, brick walls, windows and trees, but they are not proper roots, only a means of support. If these suckers come into contact with soil they will then become proper roots that can start to take in nutrients for the plant. The leaves at the base of a support usually have five lobes, but the ones in the open air at the top become a more oval shape. The berries are black with a rather pleasant odour, but taste bitter and are often used for Christmas wreaths and table decorations. Florists often use ivy leaves when they make buttonholes or posies.

If you have ivy covering walls it is best to check that you are legally allowed to remove it. Ivy provides food and shelter for many different species, including bats. If you live in the UK, you may find that you are liable to a fine if you remove ivy that has been noted as a special habitat. When I cleared ivy from dry stone walls I found that the sheep enjoyed eating it. Another reason to be careful when handling ivy is that the falcarinol in the leaves can cause dermatitis. I have only been affected by this on one occasion when I developed a rash over my upper body, which was rather unpleasant. A more likely problem for many people is the large amount of dust that is often produced when cutting back neglected ivy growth. It can get in your eyes but it also causes breathing difficulties. I now wear a dust mask if I carry out the work.

The green-yellow, nectar-rich flowers have five small petals and bloom very late in the year, providing food for insects such as hoverflies, which are increasingly hibernating later in the year as the autumn months become warmer. The leaves provide shelter for hibernating insects and birds and small animals.

The Romans made good use of ivy in their gardens. Pliny the Younger wrote a letter to Domitius Apollinaris, describing his garden where he said that:

'It is set round with plane trees covered with ivy, so that, while their tops flourish with their own green, towards the roots their verdure is borrowed from the ivy that twines round the trunk and branches, spreads from tree to tree, and connects them together.'

And Cicero wrote to his brother Quintus:

'I was able to praise your gardener. He has covered everything with ivy, the base of the villa and the spaced columns of the colonnade, so that the statues appear to be running a nursery for plants and selling ivy.'

Ivy was sacred to the Greek god Dionysius, who the Romans named as Bacchus. Both were gods of intoxication, who were often depicted with a goblet of wine in one hand and a bunch of grapes in the other. The Maenads, the female followers of Dionysus, were said to chew ivy leaves to induce intoxication and then to range across the countryside at night in a wild frenzy, tearing apart any animal or human that crossed their path; according to myth they killed Orpheus. In Euripides' play, The Bacchae, the Maenads murdered King Pentheus after he banned the worship of Dionysius. The Maenads lured him into the woods where they pulled him to pieces. One of the Maenads was his own mother, who ripped off his head in an ecstatic frenzy. The followers of Bacchus, the Bacchantes, were very similar. Both groups of followers used loud music, intoxicants and sex to free themselves from the restraints of society and their own bodies, so that they could become at one with their god. Sex and drugs and Rock 'n' Roll is nothing new! As a result, Bacchanalian is still a word that some people use to describe an orgy or a drink and drug fuelled party where anything goes.

Ivy was said to prevent drunkenness and could be worn as a wreath or more practically, boiled in wine and drunk to prevent intoxication. Culpepper gave a hair of the dog remedy for drunkenness. Drink the same sort of wine again, but this time boil the wine with some bruised ivy leaves and drink; which is rather ironic when in England, a branch of ivy used to be hung outside of a tavern to show that it sold drink.

Pliny said that the Doctrine of Signatures indicated that the yellow unripe berries were good for jaundice and Gerard said that ivy leaves soaked in water overnight could be used to help relieve watery eyes.

Ivy was considered to be a female plant. It needs to cling to something else to be able to climb, or to put it another way, it could not support itself without the help of a man. As Shakespeare wrote in *A Midsummer Night's Dream*,

'*... the Female Ivy so*
Enrings the barky fingers of the Elm.'

A weak woman, in need of a man. How things have changed from the time of the Maenads!

LETTUCE

Lettuce seems such an innocuous plant, but there is more to its story than many would imagine, as it was said to be a potent medicinal ingredient as well as being good for food. The wild lettuce, *Lactuca virosa* is now considered a weed, and it can often be found growing in the eastern and southern parts of England. It is an upright plant that usually grows to about 1m, with prickly leaves that become wider towards the tips. The flowers are yellow and similar to tiny daisies. If you break the stem or a leaf, the milky sap will flow from the wound, hence the genus name,

Genus: *Lactuca*
Species: *virosa*
Family: Asteraceae
Common Names:
  Wild Lettuce.
  Lactuca.
  Sleepwort.
  Bitter Lettuce.
  Opium lettuce.
Biennial
Active Constituents:
  Lactucopicrin.
  Lactucin.

lactuca, from the Latin word, *Lac*, meaning milk. *Virosa* means poisonous. Of all the different species of *lactuca*, the species, *virosa* is said to be the most narcotic. The extract was easily obtained by cutting off the top of plant and collecting the white sap, which was dried, during which it changed colour, becoming brown. The process could be repeated on each plant until it was finally unable to produce any more sap. The wild lettuce has a bitter flavour, but it has been cultivated since 2500 BC, when the Egyptians began to cultivate it for the leaves and the oil-rich seeds. Over the centuries, by selecting the best plants, they eventually produced a more palatable lettuce for eating. Dioscorides described the garden lettuce as having all the properties of the wild ones; the leaves cooled the stomach, but he said that the leaves should not be washed and that it was better to eat the leaves when they have been cooked. The leaves could also be used to help induce sleep. The seeds were also useful and could be preserved in brine and given to those that dreamed too much at night. The seeds could be taken to reduce male sexual desire; but there was the warning that using the seed too often risked causing dullness of sight. The Emperor Augustus gave so much credit to lettuce for saving his life from a dangerous illness that he built an altar dedicated to the plant, that even included a statue of a lettuce. Pliny said that there was a wild lettuce, called Goat- Lettuce, that when thrown into water would kill all of the fish in the area, so it is hardly surprising that it would also relieve the pain of toothache; whilst another type of lettuce was used to dye woollen cloth.

Lettuce acquired the reputation as a cure-all. It could be used as an anti-depressant, to help cure cholera, as an antidote for snake bites and poisonous waters. It improved poor eye sight, cured chest problems, eased sprains, helped stomach upsets, regulated menstruation, induced sleep, the list seems endless and in exasperation, Pliny finally remarked that he had learned of many other extravagant claims for the curative powers of the lettuce.

The *Agnus Castus Herbal* gave several uses for lettuce and described the plant as being similar to endive, but without the jagged leaf edges:

'Lettuce has a yellow flower and a tall stalk and when it is broken it drops milk. It can be eaten raw or cooked. It engenders good blood and helps women to produce milk. It is good for fevers. Simmered in vinegar with a little saffron it helps blockages of the liver and the spleen. For sleeplessness, powder the seed, add some milk from a woman and the white of an egg and make a paste and lay it on the temples and the person will soon fall asleep. A drink off the powdered seed and milk will have the same affect. Powdered lettuce seed mixed with oil of roses and laid on the stomach will destroy deep seated abscesses. The juice and /or the seed in wine cured diarrhoea.'

Throughout the early periods of Christianity, there was a fear of the succubus, a female demon that came in men's dreams at night in order to have sexual intercourse with them. This could be avoided by eating lettuce to prevent 'vain dreams', and the loss of male sperm during the night.

But vain dreams were not the only cause of blindness, because there was a warning that eating too much lettuce could also damage your eyesight and make your vison become dim. Arderne included lettuce in a sleeping ointment that must have been very effective as it included hemlock, henbane, mandrake and opium; a very powerful mix. Gerard wrote of two types of lettuce, the wild one found in the fields, and a tame one grown in gardens. Gerard thought that it was by manuring the soil and choosing the correct phase of the moon to sow the seeds that the wild lettuce would change the shape of its leaves and its form, so that the leaves may be more curled or they may fold over and become headed like a cabbage. Although Gerard never mentioned it, the curling outer leaves would stop the light reaching the inner leaves, making them paler and less bitter. The curative powers of lettuce were still being espoused; by eating lettuce, you could cool your stomach, quench your thirst and it helped to avoid drunkenness by preventing the vapours from rising to your head.

Many of us today prefer to eat lettuce raw in salads with oil, vinegar and a little salt, but Gerard agreed with Dioscorides when he suggested, that lettuce was more easily digested and provided more nourishment if it was cooked. Turner mentioned the English cabbage-headed lettuce and a spreading lettuce for eating and another third type that he named as *Lactuca sylvestris*, the Green Endive, but he then said that this plant had been incorrectly identified by the apothecaries. He was probably correct, because according to earlier herbals *Lactuca sylvestris* had purple flowers, so is more likely to be a species of thistle, and unlike the garden lettuce it had the properties of being hot and dry.

Lactuca serriola, is another wild lettuce and is the one that is thought to be the closest relative to the cultivated lettuce. The leaves are deeply cut, and on the underside, there are small spines on the mid-rib, with smaller ones along the leaf edges. The base of the leaf appears to wrap itself around the stem. The plant can be annual or biennial. Dioscorides called it *Lactuca serriola*, and said that it had the same properties as Lactuca sativa, but that the taste was very bitter. He prescribed the use as the same as for opium poppies.

Lactuca leporica is another lettuce mentioned in the early herbals. It was also known as Hare's Lettuce because the mad March hares were supposed to eat it to make themselves calm and well again. Laid on a man's side it would send him to sleep or it could be used to reduce fevers. This lettuce is most likely to be Sonchus oleraceus, the Sow Thistle. Sow thistles are eaten by many grazing animals, but were traditionally given to sows to increase their production of milk to feed their litter. A common name for Sow Thistle is Milk Thistle, but more correctly this name applies to *Silybum marianum*, a tall thistle with white markings on the leaves that are meant to remind you of the milk of the Virgin Mary. This is the thistle that is still used to make the Milk Thistle medicines that are available from chemists today.

With a long historic reputation as a soporific, it is hardly surprising to find that authors have introduced lettuce and sleep into their stories. Beatrix Potter's six young Flopsy Bunnies fall asleep after eating Mr McGregor's lettuce, making it easy for him to tie them up in a sack. They were later rescued by Thomasina Tittlemouse. Rotten vegetables were put in the sack to replace the young bunnies and Mr. McGregor went home to his wife, thinking he had six tender young rabbits for the stew pot. Edward Lear had used a similar idea for his rather morbid book, *The History of the*

Seven Families of Lake Pipple-popple, in which absolutely everybody died. The Guinea Pigs toddled about the gardens, and ate lettuces, but unlike Potter's rabbits, the seven baby guinea pigs ran headlong into the lettuce plant and were knocked out and eventually they all died of inflammation of the nose. An illustration showed seven rather tubby guinea pigs flat on their backs, unconscious under a lettuce plant.

Phillip Miller wrote several pages describing the different types of lettuce that were available for food during the late eighteenth century. The Common Garden lettuce, sometimes known as the *Laped lettuce*, was very similar to the wild lettuce and sold very cheaply. It was a loose headed lettuce used as a cut-and-come-again crop, the leaves being individually cut off when small mixed with other small salad leaves. Other named types of lettuce included, the Cabbage lettuce, the Cilicia, the Dutch Brown, the Aleppo, the Green and the Red Capuchin lettuce, the Imperial lettuce, the Roman Lettuce, the Versailles or upright white Cos, the Egyptian and the Black Cos lettuces, the Prince and the Royal lettuce. The white cos had been the favourite but the Egyptian cos was sweeter, rapidly becoming the preferred lettuce. He describes how to protect the lettuces from the cold and how, with careful management, you can have lettuce for most of the year. He went on to describe how to grow them and to save seed for the following year. One of his biggest problems was saving seed that would produce the same sort of lettuce the following year without the plants reverting back to the wild lettuce. To get good seed for the following year you should place a stick next to the best plants and allow them to go to seed, tying the stalk to a stick to prevent it being broken by the wind. When the seeds were formed, cut off the stem and lay it on muslin to dry and then beat the seeds out, allow them a little longer to dry thoroughly, after which they should be stored carefully to prevent the mice or other vermin eating them.

Today our choice of varieties of lettuce is limited. The supermarkets and restaurants prefer that we eat Iceberg lettuce, primarily because it keeps well. Cos and Romaine lettuce are still popular at the supermarket, but if you want a lettuce with a good flavour you will need to find a seed supplier who stocks the older varieties.

LILY OF THE VALLEY

For a shady area of the garden, where little else will grow, the Lily of the Valley will brighten the darkness and add a delicate heavenly scent. The species part of the name refers to the month of May, when the plant is usually in flower. The drooping white, fragrant, flowers were thought to resemble tears, but I always prefer to think of them as tiny bells. You can grow a variety of the plant with pink flowers, *Convallaria majalis* var. *rosea* if you want a change from the white flowers. In the spring, the leaves grow up

Genus: *Convallaria*
Species: *majalis*
Family: Asparagaceae
Common Names:
  Lily of the Valley.
  Our Lady's Tears.
  May Lilies.
Herbaceous Perennial
Active Constituents:
  Convallamarin.
  Convallarin.
  Azetidine-2-
  carboxylic acid.

through the soil to a height of 25cm, standing tightly folded and erect, before uncurling to reveal two leaves that are fluted so they will funnel rainwater to the base of the plant where the rhizomes are. By the autumn pale red berries are clearly visible, but few are usually produced. The seed will germinate, but it is quicker to dig up some of the rhizomes to increase your stock of plants. The rhizomes can be dug up and potted in early November and forced on indoors to provide flowers over the winter, but some say that is it unlucky to take the flowers indoors. A few flower stems will give heavenly scent to a room; I think the risk is well worth taking.

All parts of lily of the valley are poisonous. The berries are the part that is most likely to be eaten by children, but not many of them develop in most years; which is lucky, because French researchers once tested lily of the valley water on a dog by injecting four drops into a vein. It was dead within ten minutes. The symptoms of poisoning are abdominal pain, drowsiness, vomiting, reduced heart rate, blurred vision and rashes on the skin.

Brook had several uses for the flowers, which he said were one of the best medicines for the head and that they were good to remove obstructions of the urinary tracts. The powdered flowers were useful for head ache, ear ache and apoplexy, an old word used to describe what we would call a stroke. A spirit of the flowers would cure the fear of water that hydrophobics suffered from.

He provides a recipe for Etmuller's Cephalic Snuff, to induce sneezing to clear your head:

'Flowers of convallaria – one drachm
Leaves of marjoram – one drachm
Essential oil of marjoram – ten drops
Powder the leaves and flowers using a pestle and mortar and mix them together to make the snuff.

You could add a scruple of White Hellebore if you required a stronger mixture, or:

'... if the gratefulness of the smell be the object in view, a little Florentine orris-root in powder or a few grains of musk and ambergris, may be employed.'

Gerard wrote that that flowers of lily of the valley could be distilled in wine, and when given to those with the dumb palsy, they would be able to speak again. They cured apoplexy and comforted the heart. For the heart problems Gerard was correct as it has similar properties to foxgloves, and the dried flowers were still listed in the *British Pharmaceutical Codex* of 1949 for heart problems.

A cure for gout could be easily made by putting some of the flowers in a bottle, sealing the bottle and burying it in an ant hill for a month. You would find a liquid in the bottle, which could be rubbed into the affected parts of the body to relief the pain of gout. It was said to be an excellent medicine.

Coles gave a recipe for a similar medicine, known as *Aqua Aurea*, Golden Water, which was made by steeping the flowers in new wine for a month, removing the flowers and distilling the liquid three times. Coles said that the liquid was said to be so precious that it could be kept in golden or silver vessels and that the liquid itself was equally valuable as its containers.

The medicinal use of lily of the valley has mostly ceased except for homeopathy. Its main use now is for the production of essential oils to scent cosmetics and bath products; or you can simply grow the plants to decorate your garden.

MANDRAKE

andrake is now one of the best known magical plants, thanks to a certain Harry Potter. Many people think that J.K. Rowling invented the mandrake for the Harry Potter stories and that there is not a real mandrake plant, but there is, and the Bible and many herbals make mention of it centuries before Harry Potter was ever dreamed of. Mandrake's main claim to fame is that it was alleged to

Genus: *Mandragora*
Species: *officinalis*
Family: Solanaceae
Common Names:
  Mandrake.
  Satan's Apples.
Active Constituents:
  Atropine.
  Hyoscyamine.
  Scopolamine.

scream when pulled from the ground. If you heard it scream you would either die or at the very least, go raving mad. There were many ways for you to avoid death, but the most popular myth was that you should carefully loosen the roots and tie the plant to a very hungry dog; then, standing a safe distance away you would shout something along the lines of, 'Here doggy, doggy,' and produce a large bowl of food. The starving dog would then hurtle towards you and the food. The mandrake would be pulled screaming from the ground. The dog would die – and you would have a very expensive root. Nobody cared about dogs in those days! The idea of death being a major hazard of harvesting mandrakes is probably because the root would need to be about three years old to be of medicinal use. It is likely that the main purpose of the story was to scare off inexperienced collectors who may dig up juvenile plants before they were mature enough to be of practical use. It also ensured a very high price for the root.

Shakespeare, never one to miss a good tale, mentions mandrakes. Juliet recalls the tales of deadly screaming mandrakes, when she says:

'And shrieks like Mandrakes' torn out of the earth
That living mortals, hearing them, run mad.'

Gerard discounted such ideas as dreams and old wives' tales, which were completely false and untrue. He knew this because he had personally dug up and replanted many mandrake plants, as had his servants; all with no ill effect. Neither had they found any roots to which there was any resemblance to either men or women. Gerard told of another belief about the mandrake; that it was never found growing naturally, but only beneath the gallows where the matter that had fallen from a dead body has caused it to grow in the shape of a man or a woman. He was equally dismissive of this idea too.

Parkinson said that he has seen many male mandrake plants, but he had only seen a few of the female ones because they were rare and more tender and he said that they had purple flowers that appeared in August or September. He also described another species of male mandrake that he had seen with his friend, John Tradescant, at Lord Wotton's garden in Canterbury. This one had more crinkled leaves of a greyish green colour, but he couldn't describe the fruits as it seems to have never developed any. In agreement with Gerard, he added that he had dug up many mandrakes, cut the roots and replanted them; all without harm, and that the roots did not really look like a person although some did have two roots, forking in much the same way as carrots and parsnips often do. Both Gerard and Parkinson spoke of fraudulent mandrake roots, sold at great cost to those who wanted a talisman. Parkinson railed against the Chief Magistrate of the City, who appeared not to care that most mandrake roots on sale were obviously fake and being sold at great cost to the unsuspecting and credulous victims. A mandrake root does tend to fork and produce several branches, and if you have a good imagination, it may appear to have arms and legs. As for the male and female mandrakes; if you have ever seen a 'naughty carrot competition' at a garden show, I am sure that I can leave it to your imagination to work out the difference. The best root that I found had two legs and one arm. It was also a male, until a certain part of it was knocked off.

So, if you did believe the stories, why go to all the trouble of taking such elaborate precautions? The plant does have genuine useful properties. For medicinal purposes, the bark of the root was the most potent part of the mandrake, then the fruits and finally the leaves. Crescenzi said that the male and female mandrakes were not different in shape, only that the male mandrakes had longer leaves and the female ones are larger. He used both male and female plants for medicine in the same way, and gave a recipe to make oil of mandrake. Soak the apples of mandrake in oil for some time, then cook them and then allow the oil to cool and then filter it. The oil was to help induce sleep, cure headaches caused by heat and to remove the heat caused by fevers. It could also be used on hot boils.

He gave a recipe for a sleeping ointment that said that the milk of a woman who was carrying a daughter should be mixed with the powdered root bark of a mandrake and then mixed with the white of an egg. Rubbing this lotion on the patient's forehead would send them to sleep.

Mandrake's use as a sleeping draught was known to Shakespeare. When Cleopatra faced an unwanted period of loneliness, she called to her maid, Charmian:

'Cleopatra. 'Give me to drink Mandragora'.
'Charmian. 'Why, madam?'
'Cleopatra. 'That I might sleep out this great gap of time my Antony is away'.

John Arderne, the fourteenth century doctor, had a more practical use. In his book, *Fistuum in Ano*, he said that a preparation called Succus Iusquiami, could be made of mandrake, water hemlock, lettuce, and black and white poppies and 'sufficient swine's grease'. Pulverise all the ingredients in a mortar, then boil and allow to cool. If it isn't thick enough, add a little beeswax. When you need to use it, anoint the unguent to the patient's front, the pulses, temples, armpits, and the joins of his head and his feet and soon he shall sleep, so that he shall feel no cutting. It could also be used for fevers and for other cases where the patient may die if not able to sleep. Of course, if the surgery did not kill the patient, the sleeping draught may make it difficult to waken the patient. For use in a similar fashion to smelling salts, the physician could take some Grey Bread, which he toasted and soaked in strong vinegar and then held to the nose of the unconscious patient. Alternatively, mustard or vinegar could be inserted into the nostrils, or the head could be washed with strong vinegar, or you could wash the temples with rhubarb juice. Mandrake was still being used for this purpose until the introduction of modern anaesthetics, when it could be mixed with hellebore powder that would help to expel the poisons from the body by purging.

Sir Benjamin Ward Richardson was a prominent physician and anaesthetist with a keen interest in historical medical procedures. He was life-long believer in the then controversial belief of the part played by microbes in disease and personally introduced fourteen anaesthetics. In 1888, he wrote a report on some experiments that he had carried out with mandrake as an anaesthetic in the *Asclepiad,* Vol. V., under the title of *Atropa Mandragora*, which an old medical name for the plant. He had mixed crushed mandrake roots with alcohol and given the drug orally and

as an injection to pigeons and rabbits. It sent them to sleep. He tried it on his own lips, and it produced insensibility. Richardson concluded that the atropine in the mandrake was responsible and that it could be used once again as a safe way to deaden pain.

Some mandrakes flower in spring and others autumn. The plants are native to an area with hot summers, so their natural life cycle allows them to avoid being above ground at this time. The flowers tend to appear at the end of April, poking above the ground and similar in appearance to tomato flowers. My plants have flowers of a yellowy green colour, but some plants have purple flowers. The flowers are quickly followed by thin, broad leaves about 40cm long. The leaves start to die back in early summer and if the weather has been fine and warm, green tomato sized fruits develop on the surface of the soil. If the slugs do not get them first, they ripen to a pale yellow or orange colour.

The fruits have a sweet, slightly sickly scent that I find is similar to Bittersweet. Some herbals suggest that if you smell the fruits you will soon fall asleep; I have carried out experiments, but so far it has not had that effect on me.

The Carthaginian General, Hamilcar, is said to have poisoned the wine of his enemies, the Lybians, with the apples of mandrake. The Lybians became exceedingly drowsy and were then easily defeated.

The Bible suggested that mandrake was good for female fertility. Rachel wanted her sister's mandrakes so that she could carry them close to her body to help her conceive a child, so Rueben brought her sweet-smelling mandrake flowers. Gerard said that the flowers could not have been taken from mandrakes for the simple reason that the mandrake flowers do not have a delectable or amiable scent; something with which I have to agree, and Crescenzi was emphatic that mandrake would not help a woman to conceive.

Mandrakes are not a common garden plant. If you want to see one you will probably have to go to a Botanic Garden or a garden growing historical plants. The seed is available, but it is easier to germinate if it is sown when it is still fresh, so buying a plant is the easiest way to own your own mandrake.

In October 2018, Mandrake was found to have contaminated a harvest of spinach leaves in Italy, where it grows naturally. Several people were said to have been made ill and the salad bags were withdrawn from sale. Mandrake can still make the news without the help of Harry Potter.

MISTLETOE

Mistletoe is a hemiparasite, because it can carry out some photosynthesis with its own leaves, as well as taking nutrients from its host. It can be found growing on over 200 species of host plants. The green balls of mistletoe are particularly visible during the winter months when the leaves of their deciduous hosts have fallen. The white berries – botanically they are drupes – contain

Genus: *Viscum*
Species: *album*
Family: Santalaceae
Other Names:
  Mistletoe.
Evergreen Parasite
Active Constituents:
  Viscotoxins.

the seed that has a coating of viscin, a very sticky substance that ensures that the seed will remain firmly attached to any branch on which a bird has wiped its beak.

The sticky property was put to good use to make a sticky substance known as bird lime that was used not only used to trap birds that were causing damage in the garden, but also to trap small songbirds that would be eaten. Mascall repeated a recipe that he quoted from Dioscorides, for a bird lime made from mistletoe berries:

'Lime made of Misseltoo

'Dioscorides sayeth, they do gather the berries in Automne, in the full of the Moonne, (for then they are of most force) and then they broose them, and so let them lie for a space and rotte, and then they wash them in running water, till they be cleane like other lime, and therewith they do take birdes as with other birds lime made of Holly barkes.'

Mistletoe has a long history of magical use. The druids are said to have believed that mistletoe that grew on oak trees was so sacred that it could only be cut using golden sickles. This is most likely due to the rarity of mistletoe growing on oak trees, as it is more often found on hawthorn, poplar, willow and on apple trees.

Mistletoe is most commonly sold for Christmas decorations, and illegal cutting of mistletoe is now so common that on some estates gamekeepers and other workers have to patrol the trees overnight to protect their mistletoe from theft. One mistletoe custom that still thrives is that of claiming a Christmas kiss beneath a mistletoe bough hanging from the ceiling; traditionally the woman cannot refuse a kiss. One part of the tradition that is often forgotten is that after each kiss, a berry should be removed. No more berries, means no more kisses.

In Norse mythology, Baldur was the son of Odin and the goddess Frigg, and he was much loved by all. All was well until Baldur began to have dreams portending his death which caused him much worry. Odin went to the underworld to ask a deceased seeress to discover the meaning of the dreams. The seeress showed him the tables laden with food and drink for the feast to welcome Baldur once he had died. Odin returned to his home at Asgard and told Frigg what he had learned. Frigg decided that the only way to prevent Baldur's death was to ask everything in the universe not to harm him, and this is what she did. Once she had the agreement of everything in the universe the gods found great sport in throwing rocks, spears and any other dangerous object at Baldur for fun, just to see them fall harmlessly from him. Loki the mischievous trickster god, realised that this could give him an opportunity for making more trouble. He went in disguise to Frigg and asked her if she really had made an agreement with everything not to harm Baldur. 'Why yes,' she said, 'well everything except for the mistletoe which is so weak and harmless I did not worry to ask it.' Loki realised this was his moment. He went away and fashioned a sharp spear of mistletoe wood. One day, as the gods were playing their favourite sport of throwing things at Baldur, Loki approached the blind god Hodur who was all alone and left out of the entertainment. Loki offered to help Hodur to enjoy the game with the other gods and guided him to the fearless and impervious god, where he helped Hodur to aim and throw the mistletoe spear and Baldur fell dead, just as the seeress had foretold.

In a story from the Aeneid, Aeneas and Sibyl had to give a branch of the golden bough at the gates of Hades to gain entrance; mistletoe is the Golden Bough, the branches become a soft gold colour when they are dried. Sir James George Frazer must had had a similar idea in mind idea when he wrote a book on the study of magic and religion that he called, The Golden Bough. Frazer's theme was a comparative study of magic and how it evolved to eventually become formal religion. He compared myths from all around the world, showing how many were very similar. His book caused a scandal as he included Christianity, comparing the resurrection of Christ to the ancient myths of reborn fertility gods.

MONKSHOOD

Monkshood is one of the poisonous plants that many people panic about growing in a garden because of its well-publicised toxicity. It is an upright herbaceous perennial that dies down in winter. The flowers are dark blue and shaped similar to a monk's cowl or a helmet. Some species have white or yellow flowers; there are also climbing species. The name Aconitum may refer to Acone, in Asia Minor and *napellus* means small turnip, referring to the black, turnip shaped root. Another name for the plant is Wolf's Bane, as it was once used to either poison the bait you put out for wolves, or for poisoning the tips of the arrows that you intended to shoot at wolves, although *Aconitum lycoctonum* is the plant that is usually called Wolf's Bane. In a similar manner, it has been said that the Nazis put aconitine poison on their bullets during the Second World War; something that sounds more effort than it would be worth. If the story was genuinely told during the war, it is more likely to be wartime propaganda to paint as black a picture of the enemy as possible.

Genus: *Aconitum*
Species: *napellus*
Family: Ranunculaceae
Common Name:
  Monk's Hood.
  Helmet Flower.
  Wolf's Bane.
Herbaceous Perennial
Active Constituents:
  Aconitine.

Mascall provided a simple recipe for a poisoned bait to kill the vermin of England that were common in the early seventeenth century:

'Another for Rats, Mice, Woolfes, or Foxes.

Take the roote of an herbe called in latine, Aconitum: In English, Woolfes bane: and make it into a fine powder, then stowe of that powder on flesh or other thing what ye will, and it shall kill them soone after they have taken it.'

An earlier medieval recipe for a rat poison was to make a flour paste, add toasted cheese and powdered aconite and place the mixture near the rat holes.

During the early 1900s, the plant was grown commercially and collected from the wild to extract drugs. The roots were dug up during late summer and early autumn as the stems died down. The mature roots were harvested, and those that were only a year old would be replanted.

Ovid called aconite the Mother-in-Law's Poison, and centuries later, the monk Walafrid Strabo, wrote of monkshood in the same way, saying that if you suspected your step-mother of mixing poisons in your drink, or poisoning your food with lethal aconite, you should immediately take horehound as an antidote. Not that I would put much faith in surviving if you tried it.

One of the species that grows in India, *Aconitum ferox*, was used to make the poison, *Bish*, that was used to poison arrow heads. It was this plant that was involved when death by monkshood poisoning hit the British headlines in 2009, when Lakhvir Kaur Singh was tried for the murder of Lakhvinder Cheema, her lover of sixteen years. Lakhvir Kaur Singh was already married, but her marriage was not going well when she met Lakhvinder Cheema. Her excuse to visit him was that she was doing his housework to earn some extra money.

All went well until Lakhvinder Cheema met the twenty-two-year-old, Gurjeet Choongh, and very soon they became lovers. He told Lakhvir Kaur Singh that he was breaking up with her and to help get over the break-up, she went back home to India to see her family. It was a classic case of a man leaving a long-term partnership for the proverbial younger woman, whom he had intended to marry on Valentine's Day in 2009. Yet for some strange reason, Lakhvir continued to do the housework for her ex-lover. Lakhvinder and Gurjeet had a curry, Lakhvinder soon became ill and began to vomit, his face started to become numb and he began to lose his vision and the use of his limbs. His sister got the couple to a hospital, but Cheema died within an hour of arrival. Gurjeet Choongh who had the same symptoms, was put into a medically induced coma for two days and survived. Aconitine was the cause of death; Lakvir Kaur Singh had brought back some roots of Indian aconite, *Aconitum ferox*, when she returned from visiting her family a month previously and sprinkle the powdered root into the curry which had been left in a plastic box in the refrigerator. Traces of the poison were later found in Lakhvir Kaur Singh's coat pocket and handbag. She was later found guilty of the murder of her ex-lover and of grievous bodily harm in the case of Gurjeet Choongh.

The Curry Murder was the first case since of murder by aconite poisoning in England since 1882, when Dr George Henry Lamson was hanged after being found guilty of murdering his crippled brother-in-law for his inheritance. Lamson had been in the French Ambulance Corps and earned the Legion of Honour and other medals, but he had also become addicted to morphine. He had numerous debts when he decided to murder his wife's brother so that she would gain her share of his inheritance. At the Old Bailey trial, the prosecution described how Lamson had visited Percy John at his boarding school in Wimbledon. He had taken a Dundee cake as a present for the boy and slices were duly shared out. Percy died a few hours later having suffered great pain. Tests later showed that a medicinal capsule that Lamson had given the youth had included more than a lethal dose of aconite. Lamson had chosen the aconitine poison because he had been taught years before that the poison was undetectable and unknown but, unfortunately for him, forensic science had since moved on, because the poison was soon detected and he was quickly convicted.

An accidental poisoning occurred when the Canadian actor Andre Clarence Noble went on a hike on Fair Island in Newfoundland accompanied by his aunt. He was a vegetarian and a lover of nature and became unwell at his aunt's cabin on the island. He was taken by boat back to the mainland to a waiting ambulance, but died on the way to hospital. It is thought that he may have eaten berries and other plant material whilst foraging and accidentally ingested the aconitine poison by mistake. He died on 30 July 2004.

Another case of possible poisoning occurred when Nathan Greenaway, aged 33, of Aldershot, died from multiple organ failure on 7 September 2014. Nathan Greenaway worked as a gardener at Millcourt House, in Upper Froyle near Alton, Hampshire; not so far from where Jane Austen used to live. One day he was clearing weeds as he tidied the garden in readiness for a party. He complained about sickness and feeling ill when he got home when he got home and went to bed saying that he felt too weak to stand. His wife slept in a separate room so as not to catch what they both thought was a virus. She later found Nathan on the living room floor, drenched in sweat. She called for an ambulance. Initially the paramedics thought he was dehydrated, but then came a message to say that it was now an emergency case, as the doctors were concerned that Nathan could have contracted Ebola. Following an initial inquiry, Nathan's father visited the garden and discovered that monkshood grew there and he blamed the plant for his son's death. The Head Gardener, was reportedly unaware that monkshood was so dangerous, but said that the old flowering heads had been recently been pruned and he thought that it was unlikely that Nathan would have intentionally handled the plants and could have only brushed against them. The Pathologist Dr Deborah Cook said that monkshood is a common garden plant, but that few people are ever treated for aconitine poisoning. Her opinion was that there had been a very rapid deterioration of irreversible kidney and liver failure that could have been triggered by exposure to some toxin, some virus or fungus. It was noted at the time that Nathan's hands were lacerated, with the implication that he could have absorbed something into his body through the cuts. An open verdict was recorded by the coroner, Andrew Bradley, who stated that the cause of death was multiple organ failure of unknown cause. The Professional Gardeners' Guild, of which I am a member, discussed this case with great interest and concern. Many of us grew monkshood, and few of us wear gloves whilst we work; so far none of us have been affected, but I always careful to wash my hands before eating or drinking when I have been working in the garden. It is worth noting that The Royal Horticultural Society recommends that gloves be worn when handling or working with this plant. Better safe than sorry.

Parkinson was aware of the dangers of Monkshood. He described the beautiful blue flowers in fine detail, and said that they looked good in gardens and were useful to decorate windows and rooms with other flowers, yet:

> 'Beware they come not neare your tongue or lippes, lest they tell you to your cost, they are not so good as they seem to be.'

MORNING GLORY

Morning glory is a beautiful bindweed with blue flowers that continue to bloom until late autumn, but if the roots survived the winter in Britain, we would probably hate it as much as our native species. The plant is perennial in hotter climates and can be over-wintered in a pot if kept frost-free; however, most people grow new plants every year from seed.

Genus: *Ipomoea*
Species: *violacea*
Family: Convolvulaceae
Other Names:
 Morning Glory.
Tender Annual
Active Constituents:
 Ergine.
 Isoergine.
 Lysergol.

Morning glory flowers, as the name suggests, open in the morning, and in their native habitat, are pollinated by bees, butterflies and hummingbirds. One of the most popular cultivar for a garden is, 'Heavenly Blue', which has a Royal Horticultural Society Award of Garden Merit.

Morning glory seeds have a modern reputation as a legal high in many countries. Woolworths, the now defunct chain store, used to sell gardening equipment and seeds, and I remember that during the mid-1970s, they stopped selling morning glory seeds as they had heard that the local hippies were buying the seeds and taking them to get a similar effect to LSD. Woolworths were not so concerned about the LSD effect, but more of the fact that mercury based pesticides were used to protect the seeds. Mercury is not expelled from the body, so the amount of mercury in the body increases, potentially poisoning you. Most seeds are no longer coated with mercury-based pesticides and morning glory seeds are now very easy to buy again. It should be remembered that the glycosides in the seeds can cause nausea.

Morning glory, known as *tlitlitzin*, had been ingested by the priests of the South American peoples, who used its mild altering properties tribes to help them to commune with the gods and for divinatory purposes. The seeds were collected and crushed, then soaked in water, which was then drunk. Spanish chroniclers in the mid-sixteenth century reported on the divinatory use of the seeds but tried to suppress their use as being devilry because the natives believed that the god actually lived in the seeds. There are theories that suggest that the candidates for human sacrifice would be prepared with a drink of *tlitlitzin*, so that they would be impervious to the pain of having their chest cut open with an obsidian knife and their heart torn out as an offering.

The Aztec, Maya and Olmec played a ball game, Ulamaliztli, the ball being made of rubber. The sap of the rubber trees was collected from the trunks and then the sap from morning glory was added to make the rubber less brittle and more bouncy. Recent experiments have discovered that a mix of 50 per cent latex to 50 per cent morning glory sap produced balls that had a lot of bounce. The Spanish invaders wrote that the Aztec wore rubber sandals, although none have been found yet, and experiments with a 75 per cent latex to 25 per cent morning glory mix, produced a tough, hard wearing rubber that would make a good sandal. Very conveniently, the rubber trees and the morning glory usually grew close together; both plants were considered to be sacred, as was the ball game itself which may have been a symbolic battle between good and evil, with the possibility of human sacrifice being involved. It will be hard to look at the lovely blue flowers of morning glory in quite the same way again.

NETTLES

The most common stinging nettles in Britain are the perennial nettle, *Urtica dioica*, that has thick mat forming roots that make it difficult to eradicate. The other nettle is an annual plant, *Urtica urens*. Many people have heard the story that stinging nettles were introduced by the Romans so they could thrash themselves with them to get warm in the cold soggy climate of Britain. A lovely story, but that is all it is. Nettles are one of Britain's native plants. The Romans possibly did introduce a species of Nettle, *Urtica pilulifera*, which is mentioned by Gerard. The nettles would not have been introduced to keep warm for the rather obvious reason that they die down over the winter months, but they can be eaten, as long as they are cooked to prevent stinging the throat. Nettles regenerate quickly when cut back, so could provide many pickings of leaves if they were used regularly. If you do decide to eat nettles, only pick the fresh tops. The first time that I harvested nettles I did not know that, and the smell as they cooked and the taste were unpleasant to say the least; very rank and worse than over-cooked cabbage.

Genus: *Urtica*
Species: *dioica*
Family: Urticaceae
Common Names:
  Stinging Nettle.
  Stingers.
Herbaceous Perennial
Active Constituents:
Histamine.

Thankfully the nettles of Britain pack a less potent punch than *Urtica ferox*, a nettle from New Zealand which was alleged to have caused one person to die and numerous deaths of horses and dogs. The remedy in Britain for nettle stings is to rub dock leaves over the affected part of the skin. Nettles and docks both like similar growing conditions, so are often found together. I was always told to rub docks onto nettle stings to ease the pain, but I have never found it to work. Another traditional treatment is malt vinegar rubbed onto the skin that has been stung, the acidic vinegar is meant to balance the alkaline sting. When I was very young, I attempted to go around a corner far too quickly and fell off my trike into a large patch of nettles. I was wearing a T- shirt and shorts, and was stung on my face, arms, hands and legs. My mother thought that finding dock leaves would take too much time, so she used another traditional method to counter nettle stings, and washed me down with vinegar, which hurt as much as the original nettle stings.

When I first read Hans Christian Anderson's story *The Wild Swans*, in which the princess had to weave nettles into coats to break the spell on her brothers who have been turned into swans by the proverbial wicked step-mother, I thought the nettles were simply cut down and made into coats and I shuddered at the thought of wearing them and getting covered with stings, my earlier escapade with nettles still being fresh in my mind. I now know that nettle fibres have been used to make fabrics since at least the late Bronze Age. In Scotland, during the eighteenth century, the Sunday best table cloth was often made from nettle fibre; Napoleon's army uniforms were often made of nettles; modern fashion houses have experimented with nettle fibre to make jeans and jackets and since 1999, the European Union has been investigating the commercial viability of nettles as a farm crop, with the added environmental benefits to many insects, especially the Red Admiral butterfly larvae that eat the leaves. There would be a huge reduction in the amount of pesticides that would be needed, because the nettles are mostly pest-free.

Nettles have become increasingly popular in cosmetics, being included in shampoos, shower gels and hand creams. Foragers collect them to make nettle beer or to cook as vegetables. A friend once dipped the leaves in chocolate. I tried them, but you cannot taste the nettle at all.

Lightly brushing nettles is when you will receive the stinging effects most. If you want to handle nettles, grab them tightly and there is less chance of being stung. But, if you are told that stinging nettles do not sting you in months without an R in the name; do not believe it. I think it is a piece of country lore that country dwellers told the ignorant townies, for the fun of seeing them get stung.

OPIUM POPPY

The opium poppy has been used medicinally for centuries. The flower is white with a pale lilac flush and dark blotches at the base of the petals. The leaves are large, fleshy and have a glaucous colour. Walafrid Strabo wrote that the genus name came from the Latin *papare* or *pappare*, to eat or chew, from the sound of chewing the seeds. This is unlikely to be true. There are many garden varieties of the opium poppy that have brightly coloured petals or double flowers,

Genus: *Papaver*
Species: *somniferum*
Family: Papaveraceae
Other Names:
  Poppy.
  Opium Poppy.
Hardy Annual
Active Constituents:
  Morphine.
  Codeine.

whilst some resemble carnations and peonies.

The traditional method of extracting the juice was to lightly slash the seed head on the surface, but not all the way through, so the sap could run out. The sap then had to dry in the hot sun, one reason why growing your own opium in Britain has never been very successful until recently, when a new factory-based method for extracting the opiates was developed. In hotter climates, the seed heads grow much larger and produce more sap than in Britain, and it is easy to grow more than one crop per year, making opium poppies a very profitable crop in hotter climates. This may be one reason why mandrake fell out of use, as it takes at least three years to produce a good-sized root.

Meanwhile, opium poppies remain a popular garden plant, often introduced by birds from a nearby garden. They do contain a small amount of the opiates, but not enough to have been banned by law from the garden. Opium was used in England during the medieval period and John Arderne wrote that it was best to buy imported opium rather than to try to grow your own. Fields of opium poppies can now be seen growing in Wiltshire, Hampshire, Lincolnshire and Suffolk. In the UK, the poppies are harvested and baled with a combine harvester and sent off to a factory for processing, rather than each poppy seedcase being individually lanced.

Drugs wars may make the headlines today, but they are not a new phenomenon. During the eighteenth century, Britain traded with China for luxuries, including tea, porcelain and silk. China demanded payment in silver and refused to buy British goods in return. China became wealthier as Britain became poorer. At some point, somebody had the idea of growing opium poppies in India and then to illegally export opium, or to put it another way, smuggle opium into China. By the 1830s, Britain was maintaining its balance of payments for the huge amount of imports by effectively running a drugs cartel. China was gradually losing its wealth. Britain understandably wanted to make the trade legitimate and open the Chinese ports to more trade. This resulted in the Opium Wars of 1839 to 1842 and 1856 to 1860. With their superior arms and gunboats, the British forces won the day. In 1842, the Treaty of Nanking gave Britain the island of Hong Kong in perpetuity, although Britain eventually returned Hong Kong to China in 1997. The treaty also established five treaty ports at Amoy, Canton, Fuchow, Ningpo and Shanghai. The following year another treaty gave 'most favoured nation' status to the United Kingdom and added provisions for British extraterritoriality. The United States and France secured concessions on the same terms as the British in treaties of 1843 and 1844. The name Opium Wars has stuck, although the reality of the cause of the wars was a mix of imperialism, trade and the need for income. The Chinese took their revenge by exporting opium into England, where its use became entrenched across all levels of society. It made its way into many medicinal products, but it was taken as a recreational drug and also used as a means to find inspiration. During the 1800s, Wisbech and the surrounding fenlands was renowned for the high rate of opium taking and many reports were written on the subject. The Wisbech museum has a good collection of local opium pipes.

Opium was used in many different forms, but most commonly as laudanum, a mixture of opium and alcohol, usually brandy, as a pain killer and a general cure all. The poet Coleridge, used opiates to relief the pains caused by neuralgia and rheumatism. It is commonly believed that his famous poem, *Kubla Khan*, was inspired by a dream caused by the use of laudanum. He woke with the dream fresh in his mind but was disturbed by a 'person from Porlock', who had called on business, and the magical inspiration, drug induced or otherwise, was broken.

Other well-known Victorians who used laudanum as a painkiller or as a recreational drug were Lord Byron, John Keats, Percy Shelley, Elizabeth Barrett-Browning, Charles Dickens, George Eliot, Elizabeth Gaskell, Gabriel Dante Rossetti and his wife Lizzie Siddal, who died in 1862 as a result of an overdose of laudanum. Bram Stoker also took laudanum, which may help to explain the inspiration for his book, *Dracula*. Lord Byron's daughter, Ada Lovelace, was a mathematical genius and the first person who could be described as a computer programmer. She was prescribed laudanum for asthma and then became addicted to it.

Children were given 'Godfrey's Cordial' which contained opium to help them sleep, which was not a new use because one medieval herbal had already passed on a similar tip, when it said that during the medieval period Italian women would make poppy head tea to help their noisy, crying children go to sleep at night. A few years ago, I met a Frenchwoman in her seventies who told me that her mother used to make her drink poppy head tea to help her sleep. Thankfully, she appeared to have suffered no ill-effects. I have since met many people from the Fens who have told me tales of poppy head tea still being used today, but mainly for recreational use. Opiates were used to treat many other ailments including, hiccoughs, colic, diarrhoea, vomiting, pleurisy, rheumatism, catarrh, rheumatism, 'women's troubles' and coughs. The most potent cough medicine recipe that I have seen was called One Night Cough Syrup. It contained alcohol, cannabis, chloroform and morphine. It might not cure the cough, but you would not care anyway.

The active constituent in opium, morphine, was first extracted by the German chemist Friedrich Sertner, in 1805. It has been used as a medicine ever since.

On the 10 April 1917, Siegfried Sassoon complained of a sore throat, gastritis and festering cuts on his hands. He also complained that he had no clean handkerchiefs nor socks, but he consoled himself with an enormous opium pill to induce constipation, as he says, with a subtle turn of phrase, 'suitable for open warfare.' A very practical use of the drug by a soldier to induce one of opium's well-known side effects – constipation.

Opium Poppy seeds are still used to decorate and flavour bread and cakes. The seeds themselves do not contain morphine, but they can become contaminated if the juice is absorbed during harvesting. The US Anti-Doping Agency (USADA) website recommends avoiding poppy seed consumption before and during competitions. A test performed in Germany in 2003 by the Institute of Biochemistry found that people who ate a popular poppy seed cake still had traces of opiates in their blood after forty-eight hours; some as high as 10 microg/ml. At the time, the International Olympics Committee had recognised that a positive result was 1 microg/ml. There are many recorded cases of people losing their jobs from similar drugs tests; some were later reinstated once the problem caused by poppy seeds was recognised. I heard of a lorry driver who had failed a routine drink and drugs test at work when minute traces of opiates were found in his blood sample. He denied using the drug and wondered how the opiates found their way into his sample. He then remembered that he ate a large amount of poppy seed bread. Having removed the bread from his diet, no more opiates were discovered in future blood samples.

If you are affected by opium, a medical book of the 1747 said feverfew was a good antidote to both opium and henbane. Another antidote that probably does not work.

PASQUE FLOWER

Pasque flower prefers to grow in the turf of alkaline fields, but is now rare in Britain, growing mostly in Cambridgeshire, Gloucestershire, Hertfordshire, Lincolnshire, Oxfordshire and Wiltshire. Gerard said that that the common name of pasque flower was simply due to the time that it usually flowered, which is during the Easter period. The vulgaris part of the name means common, but in this particular case the name is misleading because of its rarity. Another common name is Dane's Blood, because it often grew on the old earth banks of hill forts where the invading Dane's had been defeated. It grows to about 20cm or slightly higher and has purple flowers, although sometimes they are closer to red. There is a white flowered pasque flower, of which Gerard said that the leaves looked rather like holy water sprinklers. The stems and leaves have fine, silky hairs and

Genus: *Pulsatilla*
Species: *vulgaris*
Family: Ranunculaceae
Other Names:
  Pasque Flower.
  Meadow Anemone.
  Dane's Blood.
  Passe Flower.
Herbaceous Perennial
Active Constituents:
  Ranunculin.

the seed heads are round and also covered with hairs. A green dye from the stems has been used in some European countries to paint hen's eggs at Easter.

Poisoning is rare, probably because the plant is, and you would need to eat a lot of leaves for the dose to be fatal. The taste of the leaf is like buttercup petals and quite bitter; it made my tongue tingle for some time after when I tried it. The effect of the toxins is said to be similar to that of aconites, with a slow pulse, slow breathing, loss of body temperature and paralysis.

Gerard said that the juice could cause ulcers on the skin, whilst Parkinson said that the distilled water could be used for malarial fevers and as a powerful medicine to remove obstructions. Pasque flower was once thought to be an anemone and could have similar properties, but most herbals ignore it. I agree with Gerard, who said that:

'There is nothing extant in writing of authors of any particular virtue, but they serve only for the adorning of gardens and garlands, being flowers of great beauty.'

PHEASANT'S EYE

donis annua grows to a height of about 30cm. It has fine foliage, rather like chamomile, Gerard said, which is a good description. The flowers are a bright red, and usually bloom from May to August, depending on when the seed was sown. Gerard said that the flower was a common weed of cornfields in the West Country, and that is where he went to collect seed so he could grow the flower in his London

Genus: *Adonis*
Species: *annua*
Family: Ranunculaceae
Other Names:
  Pheasant's Eye.
Hardy Annual
Active Constituents:
  Adonidin.
  Aconitic acid.

garden. The plant is now rare in Britain, being mostly found in the south, but seed is widely available.

The medicinal use by the ancients, as Gerard called them, was limited to using the seed to help with kidney stones. Gerard added that in his time the seed was powdered and given in ale, beer or wine for colic. It has been used as a cure for dropsy and heart problems in a similar way to foxgloves. All parts of the plant are poisonous, with toxic effects being similar to digitalis, by affecting the action of the heart. It is also said to be a laxative and diuretic, but it is not a plant to be used for self-medication.

In Greek mythology, Adonis was a beautiful youth, who captured the heart of Aphrodite. Adonis was attacked and killed by a wild boar, possibly arranged by Artemis or another version of the story said it was Aphrodite's lover, who was jealous of Adonis. Adonis died in Aphrodite's arms, and in her grief, she mixed his blood with nectar and sprinkled it over the ground, from which anemones grew, but several plants with red flowers are associated with the blood of Adonis. One of the mystery cults of ancient Greece was based around the tale of Adonis.

PETTY SPURGE

Petty Spurge is a common weed in many gardens, although there are garden plants of the same genus. It is an annual that has an irritant white sap that is common to most euphorbias. Any plant called a spurge is likely to have been one of the medicinal purging plants.

The weed may be a fairly insignificant plant, but it was at the centre of the Great Plague

Genus: *Euphorbia*
Species: *peplus*
Family: Euphorbiaceae
Common Names:
  Spurge.
Hardy Annual
Active Constituents:
  Aesculetin.

of Nassington, of 1895, although you have probably never heard of it. Nassington is a large village not far from Fotheringhay in Northamptonshire, that once had a Royal Manor that later became a Prebendal Manor owned by the church. The plague was first noticed during the summer at the village school. Children were developing rashes on their faces, legs, arms and hands. Parents, worried that there may be a contagious disease that was being spread amongst the children when they were as the school, began to keep their children at home. The Headmaster was worried and called in the Medical Office from the nearby town of Oundle. The official spent a day at the school, to inspecting the children, and trying to discover the cause for the rash. He had reached two conclusions. Firstly, that there was no Great Plague, as there was definitely no infectious disease and that the children should return to school immediately. Secondly, the rashes, some as large as a half crown, (a coin around one and one eighth of an inch across), were self-inflicted. He said that the children had collected a local plant known as Patty Spurge and rubbed the irritant juice onto their faces and hands to cause the rashes to avoid going to school. The newspaper report said that once the parents realised the truth that several children were known to have received a severe beating. Needless to say, there has never been another outbreak of plague at Nassington. Beggars in India and other countries still use the juice of their native euphorbias rubbed onto their limbs and faces to induce rashes in order to gain greater sympathy from passers-by in the hope that they will receive more sympathy, and money, from passers-by.

RUE

R ue is an evergreen plant with bi, or tri-pinnate leaves of an attractive glaucous colour, although they have a strong scent and a very bitter taste; the flowers are yellow, although rather small, helping to make rue a good garden plant, although it can be difficult to obtain from a general garden centre.

Rue is another of the plants introduced by the Romans into Britain from the Mediterranean.

Genus: *Ruta*
Species: *graveolens*
Family: Rutaceae
Common Names:
  Holy Herb of Grace.
  Rue. Herbygrass.
Evergreen Shrub
Active Constituents:
  Furocoumarins.

Rue prefers free draining soil and will survive cold conditions providing the roots are not waterlogged. The plant can withstand severe clipping, making it useful in the past for the low hedging of knot gardens. Rue is easy to grow from seed or cuttings and if the soil is suitable the plant will happily self-seed around the garden or in dry-stone walls.

Rue is mentioned by Pliny, who told how the roman slaves would be sent out to collect lots of rue branches which would be tied in bunches and hung in the villa windows to deter the flies; even today, some people still use rue leaves to deter flies and ants, whilst some herbals say that rue can also be used to kill fleas. Pliny is probably the first person to record one of the major problems of rue, that in bright sunlight it causes similar photochemical burns to those of the giant hogweed.

Rue was considered a magical plant that could give protection from witchcraft. Priests would dip branches of rue in Holy Water to sprinkle about to disperse evil and purify the church before High Mass on Sundays. It was thought that retention of sperm in the body would cause illness and Hildegard said that if a man became stirred in lust to the point that his sperm was at the point of emission, but remained in his body, he could become ill. To cure the problem, the man should take some rue and a little less wormwood and squeeze out the juice from them and in a new pot, add sugar, honey and wine and heat the mix by inserting a hot poker five times and drink the liquid whilst it is still warm after a meal, and according to Hildegarde, 'the noxious liquid will pass out of him with his urine'. A contrary use of rue was to protect men from the female devil known as an incubus, but also called the mare, who tried to have sexual intercourse with men in their dreams, so the Physicians of Myddfai said that if you wish to preserve yourself from unchaste desires, you should eat rue in the morning.

Rue could also be used as a pessary or the juice can be taken orally, to remove a dead child from the womb or to bring on the menses. The plant has a very bitter taste and in the past, it has been used for medicines to be taken internally, but nowadays it is not recommended for consumption. Gerard said that rue was a good antidote to the poisons from wolf's bane, mushrooms, toadstools, snake bites, scorpions, spiders and stinging insects and if you rubbed onto the body, they would not be able to hurt you.

Rue was also one of the herbs that judges carried in their posies at court to help protect them from gaol fever, nowadays known as typhus, spread by the bites of fleas. The scent of the rue was meant to discourage fleas and thus protect the judge. The judge could also inhale the scent of the posy to help disguise the general stink of the crowded courts.

I have met a woman who suffered from rue as she brushed past the plant on a hot sunny day. The plant had formed seed cases and these seem to cause worse burns than those of the leaves. She soon developed blisters and swellings that hurt and then needed medical attention. Initially she thought that the problem had been caused by her euphorbias and had taken a stem to the hospital with her. The doctors checked the symptoms on a database and soon realised that the euphorbias were not to blame. Her case was so serious that the hospital took photos of her body as a record of how it had reacted to the plant and sent out the pictures to other hospitals so they would recognise the signs if anybody else reported similar symptoms. A similar case had been reported at another hospital where they were unsure as to the cause of their patient's suffering, but once they saw the photos they quickly diagnosed the problem.

A recipe for pain of the eyes was to fill an egg shell with the juice of fennel, rue, clarified honey, wine and the urine of a child. You should anoint the eye with the mixture using a feather. In view of the risks from rue, it is probably better to go to the opticians for some modern eye drops.

SAVIN

avin is a hardy evergreen shrub. There are usually separate male and female plants, but sometimes a plant will produce male and female flowers on different branches. The berry-like fruits can take over a year to ripen to a dark blue/black colour and have a bloom like a plum, and contain small seeds, usually not more than three. The very thin leaves are very prickly when handled. The plant takes three main forms: a low growing shrub that can be nearly 3m in diameter but less than a metre tall, which rarely produces berries; the upright savin can grow to nearly 3m tall and will bear many berries; and there is a low growing, variegated savin, but I have only seen few attractive specimens. Some books describe the low growing plant as male because it rarely produces berries in Britain. The upright savin produces berries quite easily, so was often described as the female plant, although in reality, they are not the same plant. Savin was used in English gardens for topiary but I do not like pruning it as the needles get stuck in your clothing and cause scratches and itching. Some garden books suggest that the smell as a good reason not to grow savin in the garden, unless it is the variegated one.

Genus: *Juniperus*
Species: *sabina*
Family: Cupressaceae
Common Names:
   Savin.
Evergreen Shrub
Active Constituents:
   Sabinene.
   Sabinol.
   Terpinine.
   Thujone.

Parkinson wrote that clothing would often be laid over savin bushes to dry; one reason being to give the clothing a good scent, another to kill bugs. The oil could be rubbed onto children's bellies to kill worms. But Savin and juniper were more widely known as powerful abortifacients. Gerard knew of the abortifacient properties, but he suggested that men who had been with unclean women and now had growths under the foreskin, known as caroles, could dry savin leaves and then crush them to a fine powder, which would cure the problem and leave the skin perfectly clean.

Coles called the plant as offensive to conception. Brooks was certainly aware of the uses and the dangers of savin:

'Those miserable women who take it for a certain purpose, little know the danger of the practice – destroying the constitution, and in many cases producing instant death.'

SOAPWORT

oapwort will grow to a height of 70cm, but you will rarely find it actually growing at that high, whether in the garden or the wild, as it tends to flop onto the ground, hence one of its common names, Bouncing Bet. The lightly scented flowers have five petals, usually white, but they can be found in shades of pink. A double form is often grown in gardens. The plant spreads

Genus: *Saponaria*
Species: *officinalis*
Family: Caryophyllaceae
Other Names:
    Soapwort.
    Bouncing Bet.
Herbaceous Perennial.
Active Constituents:
    Saponarin.

through a vigorous root system and by seed, rapidly covering large areas of ground unless kept firmly under control. The roots and the leaves both contain saponins that can make you ill if swallowed, but they create a cleansing soap that was traditionally used to clean clothing. The roots can be dug up and dried for later use and have the advantage on not containing any chlorophyll which can stain some clothing. By digging up the roots you can keep the plant growing within bounds. I have been demonstrating the soap properties for years. I usually use the leaves, picking off a few, immersing them in water and rolling them between the palms of my hands, which quickly produces a froth of green lather. The soap is one of the softest that you can obtain and has been used to clean old textiles, even those dating from the fifth to seventh centuries in Egypt. The method is usually by soaking the supported textiles on a frame and immersing them in a soapwort solution, leaving them to soak and then rinsing them several times. Although this method is still used on mainland Europe, recent research at Hampton Court has led to using manufactured soaps that are better than soapwort.

I have washed my hair using soap from the leaves. There are no bubbles as there are with modern shampoos, but your hair will be cleaned. I have also made my own concentrated liquid soap by simmering lots of leaves in a large pan of water, then leaving it to stand overnight and slowly simmering the liquid to reduce the water content. It kept for several years until I had used it all. Saponaria is still used in some commercial cosmetic products. Expensive hand creams often include it as a skin softener and I have seen it as an ingredient of shampoos.

SEA SQUILL

Drimia maritima, named as *Urginea maritima* in older books, is a bulbous Mediterranean plant that grows on the dry, sandy areas but also inland. It is often said that it was first cultivated in England at Oxford Botanic Gardens in 1648, but Parkinson says that he and others had been sold bulbs by mariners for their use. It seems odd that they did not try to grow them. The bulbs can become quite large, sometimes weighing up to two kilograms; Parkinson said he had seen bulbs the size of a child's head. He says that the Spanish would not let Clusius even

Genus: *Drimia*
Species: *maritima*
Family: Asparagaceae
Common Names:
  Red Squill.
  White Squill.
  Sea Squill.
  Sea Onion.
  Sea Hyacinth.
Bulb.
Active Constituents:
  Scilliroside.

taste a red bulb as it was so poisonous. He then says that the bulb is not grown in gardens as the flower was not considered attractive. The leaves rise from the base of top of the bulb and are hollow. The bulb of Europe plants is usually white; African bulbs tend to be red. Bulbs of both colours have similar properties and have been used for medical purposes but also to kill rats. Charlemagne called *Urginea, Scilla-de-morts-aux-rats*, which is rather self-explanatory. Most older books recommend the red bulbs for rodenticides, being especially useful on farms as it does not affect cattle or pigs. It seems that in reality it makes little difference which colour bulb you use to kill rats as long as you are careful where you place the bait, and the bulb continued in use as a rodenticide until the 1950s. Modern research has shown that red squill powder is three to four times more lethal for female rats than for male rats.

Dioscorides gives squill as an *alexipharmacon*, that is an antidote to poison, and that it should be hung up whole before the door. He describes the process by which it should be prepared or dried. He mentions that the sharp, burning property can be removed by wrapping the bulb in dough or clay and roasting it under hot coals. If the bulb is thoroughly cooked it will be safe to eat. The middle and outer parts can be removed, then cut the bulb into pieces and cover them with water and allow the pieces to soak for some time. Throw away the water and cover with fresh water and repeat until the water is no longer sharp and bitter to taste. The pieces can now be strung onto a linen thread, being careful not to let the pieces touch each other then they can be hung in the shade until dry. For medicinal purposes, the bulb could be dried, made into a treacle or syrup, or soaked in wine or vinegar. The *Agnus Castus Herbal* gives Squill as a cure for the bites of adders and other venomous beasts and to make a person sick.

More recently, the bulb was usually imported as dried slices. The outer scales were removed and the bulb was cut into very thin slices and dried. Once dried the root had to be kept in a sealed container as it would quickly absorb moisture. If kept dry, the slices could be easily made into powder, but if they became moist they would become quite tough. Squill was used for coughs, as a diuretic, for dropsy, a cardiac as it has similar effects as digitalis, but it was also used as a purge. It was often administered with opium to counter act its effect on the stomach. The *Trotula* said that women who wanted to remove abscesses from the face after having given birth should smear their face with squill, which would cause the skin to raise. The face should then be rubbed with goat tallow to remove the raised skin.

The bulb is available from specialist bulb growers, although it is not completely hardy in Britain and needs to be taken indoors over winter.

STRYCHNINE

Nux vomica is found in India and Malaya. It is not generally grown in Britain, even at Kew; only the Chelsea Physic Garden seem to grow a related species. The earliest known member of the family is *Strychnos electri,* being at least fifteen million years old. It was discovered in a mine in the Dominican Republic, as a flower, perfectly preserved, embedded in amber, by entomologist George Poinar, in 1986. The lack of plants growing in Britain was never a

Genus: *Strychnos*
Species: *nux vomica*
Family: Loganiaceae
Common Names:
  Strychnine.
  Poison Nut.
  Semen strychnos.
  Quaker Buttons.
Tender Evergreen Shrub
Active Constituents:
  Strychnine.

problem for medical practitioners as the large, round, seeds were very easy to transport.

The name of the plant literally means the 'vomiting nut' and reflects its main medicinal use as a purge. The seeds have been imported into Britain since at least the Tudor period, if not before. *Nux vomica* is mentioned in the *Herbal* of Rufinus as good for helping to balance the phlegm and choleric humours whilst the Syon *Herbal* only includes *Nux vomica* as a purge for choler. It was a medicine that had to be used with great caution.

Another traditional use has been to poison rodents, with many early rat poisons containing strychnine. A later use for strychnine was to kill moles. Earthworms were soaked in a strychnine solution and then put into the mole runs for the moles to eat, but as moles prefer live worms, it may not have been very successful. No matter what the success rate was, following a British appeal by the British government on behalf of the 3,000 licenced users, the European Health and Safety Executive declared that strychnine should be banned for poisoning moles on environmental grounds.

Mascall used *nux vomica* as the toxic ingredient to poison ravens, crows and magpies. He made note of the fact that not all poisons affect each species in the same way, when he seemed to offer a personal observation that kites would not usually keep the poison down and so escaped the harmful effects:

'To take Ravens, Pyes and Crowes

'You shall take of Nux vomica, so called, which ye shall buy at the Apothecaries, they are gathered by the sea, and are as broed as a piece of foure pence, and a quarter of an inch thicke, or more. Those which are the whitest within, are counted for the best, when ye will ocupye any doe (Illegible) or cut one smalle in thinne pieces, then beate it into powder if ye can the finer it is the better, and the sooner will make the Crowes or Pyes to fall. Put of the sayd powder into a piece of flesh, and so lay it abroad, and yee shall soon see Pie, or Crowe or Raven take it. Then must you watch him a while after, and ye shall perceive him to fall downe, then must ye follow to take him. But if yee let him remaine one quarter of an hour, he will recover againe, for this nux vomica it doth but make them drunk, and dyzie for a time. The Kyte I have not seene taken, for he will cast it up againe.'

It was not until 1818 that the chemists Pelletier and Caventou, separated the active compound strychnine, from the seed of *Strychnos ignatia*, the St Ignatius Bean, as a white crystalline substance. It was later extracted from *Strychnos nux vomica*. The reason strychnine was used to kill rodents, and

people, was that it was cheap, and easily bought from a druggist for eight pence an ounce.

Strychnine has been described as the poison that kills you and leaves you with a smile on your face, but this greatly underplays the true effect of the poison. Strychnine can cause very violent muscle contractions, enough to make the body to bend back to an unnatural degree before the victim finally dies of asphyxiation. It is particularly horrible for the victim as they will remain conscious throughout the ordeal. Strychnine was the poison that Norman Bates chose to poison his mother, in Alfred Hitchcock's film *Psycho*. It would have been easy to obtain and one third of a grain can lead to death within twenty minutes.

TANSY

Tansy grows to a height of 100 to 150cm. The green leaves are alternate, finely divided with a fern-like appearance and have a strong pungent scent. The stem is stiff and bears most of the leaves towards the top. The button-like flowers are yellow and carried as flat-topped clusters at the end of the stems; they have the same scent as the leaves. The stems can be cut late summer and dried for indoor floral displays. The plant can

Genus: *Tanacetum*
Species: *vulgare*
Family: Asteraceae
Common Names:
   Tansy.
   Batchelors Buttons.
Herbaceous Perennial
Active Constituents:
   Thujone.

spread rapidly in good garden soil and as Parkinson said, the roots creep underground and shoot up again in diverse places. Be warned. I have seen tansy growing wild by streams and ditches in the Lake District, but they may have been garden escapes.

The Plan of St Gall includes tansy in its garden and Strabo, writing at about the same date, says that tansy is also called *Ambrosia* in reference to the food of the Olympian gods that gave immortality, although the name tansy is thought to derive from *Athanaton*, another Greek word for immortality. According to a legend, Gannymede ate *Athanaton* to make himself immortal.

Strabo said that a draught of tansy would clear as much blood away from inside you as the dose that you drink. Macer passed over tansy in seven lines, saying that it had a bitter taste and many virtues being that it purged the breast and all parts within the body. He actually wrote more words in apology because he had not written much about tansy! Gerard said that the root could be preserved in honey or sugar to treat gout.

The main use for tansy was as a vermifuge to remove intestinal worms. Parkinson said that during Lent and spring the juice of tansy and other such herbs was mixed with eggs and fried to make *Tansies* to help remove the bad humours that resulted from the fast of Lent. The bitter taste was also said to commemorate the bitter herbs that the Israelites were forced to eat at the Passover.

Mrs. Grieves gave the following recipe for making a Tansy:

'Beat seven eggs yolks and whites separately. Add a pint of cream, about the same of spinach-juice and a little tansy juice, a quarter of a pound of Naples biscuit, sugar to taste, a glass of white wine, and some nutmeg. Set all in a sauce-pan, just to thicken, over a gentle heat, then put it into a dish, lined with paste, to turn out, and bake it.'

The leaves have been used to repel insects, making it a useful addition to the strewing herbs. Due to its toxic properties, tansy had another use, to induce abortions, but Culpepper had the opposite in mind when he wrote:

'Let those Women that desire Children love this herb, 'tis their best companion, their Husband excepted.'

THORN APPLE

Unravelling the historical references to datura and linking it to the correct species is complicated. The descriptions of plants given in early writings are not always very informative. Botanical experts have many different theories on whether *Datura stramonium* was known in Europe, Africa and Asia before the discovery of America. Datura seed remains viable for about ten years and have been carried by travellers, so that *Datura stramonium* has now colonised

Genus: *Datura*
Species: *stramonium*
Family: Solanaceae
Common Names:
  Thorn Apple.
  Jimson Weed.
Annual
Active Constituents:
  Hyoscyamine.
  Atropine.
  Scopolamine.

many parts of the world since it escaped from America – if it did in fact, escape.

Some academics claim that Datura is mentioned in Dioscorides under the name of *Struchnon Manikon*, but Dioscorides description of the plant does not match *Datura stramonium*:

'It sends out 10 or 12 tall stalks from the root, having the height of an ell. The flower is black, and after this it has a fruit, cluster-like, round, black, partitions 10 or 12, like the corymbi of ivy, soft as a grape.'

This seems to represent a solanum with soft berries, rather than a plant with a hard, spiky seed case. *Datura metel* is often credited as the plant most likely to have been known to the Old World inhabitants. It contains all the toxic properties of the rest of the datura family and has the benefit of sweetly scented flowers which could encourage its being grown for decoration as well as for medicinal and other purposes.

William Turner made no mention of datura of any species. Anne van Arsdall said that Thorn Apple was included in the *Old English Herbarium*, but the *Herbarium* does not include a description of the plant, so all we are given is a name, *trychnos manicos* (more accurately strychnos from Dioscorides) or *Foxes Glofa*, with the note that the name, foxglove, was used for other poisonous plants, which sounds rather tenuous.

Gerard gave a very accurate description of thorn apple and said that the plant causes drowsiness. He commented that the plant was rare in England and that he had received his seed from John Robin of Paris. He mentioned that Lord Edward Zouche had brought back some seeds of another species of thorn apple from Constantinople that he gave to Gerard, which he had grown and had also given to others. He used the plant for burns, scalding, and malign ulcers. The flowers were white and sweetly scented, and he noted that the plant only lived for a year. In this particular case, he could possibly be referring to Datura metel, as the flowers of thorn apple could hardly described as being sweetly scented.

He explained that the first early sowing of the seeds should be made on a hot bed. This was an early method of warming soil to start crops early and extend them later in the year. Fresh manure would be piled and flattened and covered with a soil to about six inches deep and a wooden frame with glass placed over the top. Seeds could be sown inside or plants grown to protect them from the cold.

Gerard claimed that thorn apple in hog's grease made a salve that would help for all types of burns and scalds; even from gun powder, boiling lead and even lightning. He cured the wife of a merchant, Mistress Lobel of Colchester, who was struck by lightning. She was completely cured by this salve when everything else had failed and all hope was past.

Parkinson listed several species of datura said that all the *Datura* species were introduced into England from Turkey and Egypt, but that Garcias and Christopher Acosta had confirmed that they also grew in the East Indies.

Garcia de Orta, c.1501-68, was a doctor who experimented with medicine, rather than just acting on the traditional uses. He wrote *Colóquios dos simples e drogas he cousas medicinais da Índia*, which was the first European book to be written on the medicinal and practical uses of Indian plants. Christophorus Acosta Africanus, c.1525-c.1594, was a

Portuguese doctor who had travelled to the East Indies. He wrote that:

> 'The East Indian lascivious women performe strange acts with the seed (of the smaller kinde, as I suppose, or it may be of either) giving it their husbands to drinke.'

This would suggest that it was being given as an aphrodisiac, but Parkinson also describes how the plant can send people to sleep and that it may be useful for surgeons, if used with caution, when they carry out operations to an arm or a leg or even for cutting open the body to remove stones.

The Physicians of Myddfai said that thorn apple could be applied to teeth to stop them aching. As many of the recipes were written down in the fourteenth century, some people have said that this proves that thorn apple was known in Britain during the medieval period, but the last physician died in 1739, so this recipe is more likely to be a later addition.

Thorn apple is sometimes known as Jimson Weed, a corruption of James Town, the first English colony in America. In 1679, English soldiers at Jamestown ate some Jimson Weed leaves in a salad. It is not known if this was intentional, or whether the food had been 'spiked' by persons unknown. A few years later in 1705, Robert Beverley wrote an account of the outcome in his *History and Present State of Virginia*:

> 'The *James-Town* Weed (which resembles the Thorny Apple of *Peru*, and I take to be the Plant so call'd) is supposed to be one of the greatest Coolers in the World.
>
> This being an early Plant, was gather'd very young for a boil'd Salad, by some of the Soldiers sent thither, to pacific the Troubles of *Bacon*; and some of them eat plentifully of it, the Effect of which was a very pleasant Comedy; for they turn'd natural Fools upon it for several Days: One would blow up a Feather in the Air; another wou'd dart Straws at it with much Fury; and another stark naked was sitting up in a Corner, like a Monkey, grinning and making Mows at them; a Fourth would fondly kiss, and paw his Companions, and snear in their Faces, with a Countenance more antick, than any in a *Dutch Droll*. In this frantick Condition they were confined, lest they should in their Folly destroy themselves; though it was observed, that all their Actions were full of Innocence and good Nature. Indeed, they were not very cleanly; for they would have wallow'd in their own Excrements, if they had not been prevented. A Thousand such simple Tricks they play'd, and after Eleven Days, return'd to themselves again, not remembring any thing that had pass'd.'

Brook says that thorn apple had been 'an assistant to the incantations and the unlawful practices of witches' during the English Civil War period. He then recommended that nobody should use the plant for medicine without first taking the very best medical advice.

Thorn apple may have been used as an aphrodisiac. In May 2010 an art historian, David Bellingham, offered a new interpretation of a painting in the National Gallery. The painting by the fifteenth century artist, Botticelli, usually known as *Venus and Mars*, shows Venus and Mars relaxing in a rural setting after an adulterous liaison; Venus was already the wife of the god of fire, Vulcan. The painting has been thought to represent the power of love to civilise; but obviously whilst discounting the not so civilised behaviour of the adultery involved.

David Bellingham noticed that a satyr, shown in the lower right corner, appeared to be resting his hand on the thorn covered seed case of *Datura stramonium*. Bellingham suggested that Venus and Mars have used the plant as an aphrodisiac, although the look on Venus' face appears to show disappointment, so maybe Mars took the plant to improve his ardour, but used too much of the drug and fell asleep. Meanwhile, in the background three more satyrs are playing with his helmet and lance as Mars slumbers. I am not convinced that the seed case is a datura at all. If you enlarge the painting, there are not any prominent thorns as there would be on a thorn apple seed case. Other suggestions include *Ecballium elaterium*, the squirting cucumber, the fruit of which if touched when it is ripe, powerfully squirts out the seed – so a good sexual pun for an adulterous liaison. The plant was also used as an abortifacient, so another practical use for a married lover.

In the USA in 1994, two boys, aged sixteen and seventeen died after consuming a drink brewed from the roots of thorn apple and other alcoholic drinks, two others who also drank the brew survived, suffering only from hallucinations. Another case involved a man of eighteen, who had eaten fifty thorn apple seeds, cannabis, cocaine and Ecstasy was found naked and suffering hallucinations, but he survived.

Thorn apple is related to the angels trumpets, once known as *Datura* but now classified as *Brugmansia*. In the UK, angels' trumpets are a tender perennial, so they need protection from frosts over the winter. The flowers can be up to 10cms long and produce a very sweet and intoxicating scent. The plant is toxic, although many years ago the Sunday papers often included a copy of a plant catalogue, which showed a picture of a young child sweetly and innocently, smiling up into a flower to give an indication of how large the flowers would be, but with no suggestion that the plant is poisonous.

TOBACCO

Tobacco is a very easy plant to grow, and besides the species grown for the leaves to produce tobacco, there are many that are grown as decorative plants in the garden. When I was younger it was perfectly legal to grow your own tobacco for smoking. Many of the allotment plots in the village had a good area planted with tobacco. The leaves were harvested and sent off for processing. In return for which, the allotment holders received

Genus: *Nicotiana*
Species: *rustica/tabacum.*
Family: Solanaceae
Common Names:
   Tobacco.
   Nicotiana.
Tender Annual
Active Constituents:
   Nicotine.

properly processed tobacco that they could smoke.

Tobacco is only mentioned in herbals that date from the Elizabethan period onwards. It was named after the Frenchman, Jean Nicot, 1530-1600, a French agent working in Portugal who introduced tobacco into France. Traditionally in Britain, Francis Drake is credited with the introduction of tobacco and smoking in 1570. The earliest description of tobacco is in a book of 1569, by Nicolas Monardes, *Dos libros el veno que trata de todas lascosas que traen de nuestras Indias Occidentles*. John Frampton published a translation in 1569 that included the first illustration of a tobacco plant. His book was titled, *Joyfull newes out of the new founde Worlde*, which is rather ironic in view of the many deaths that tobacco would cause.

The natives of Virginia were noted for their use of tobacco and smoking as a way of distinguishing friends and enemies. Or allowing safe passage through unknown lands. The following explanation is from *Virginia book on natives and tobacco*:

'They have a peculiar way of receiving Strangers, and distinguishing whether they come as Friends or Enemies; tho they do not understand each others Language: and that is by a singular method of smoaking Tobacco; in which these things are always observ'd.

'1. They take a Pipe much larger and bigger than the common Tobacco Pipe, expressly made for that purpose, with which all Towns are plentifully provided; they call them the Pipes of Peace.

'2. This Pipe they always fill with Tobacco, before the Face of the Strangers, and light it.

'3. The chief Man of the Indians, to whom the Strangers come, takes two or three Whiffs, and then hands it to the chief of the Strangers.

'4. If the Stranger refuses to Smoke in it, 'tis a sign of War.

'5. If it be Peace, the chief of the Strangers takes a Whiff or two in the Pipe, and presents it to the next Great Man of the Town, they come to visit; he, after taking two or three Whiffs, gives it back to the next of the Strangers, and so on alternately, until they have past all the persons of Note on each side, and then the Ceremony is ended.

This Method is as general a Rule among all the Indians of those parts of America, as the Flag of Truce is among the Europeans.'

Along with sugar cane, tobacco is probably responsible for funding the building of many of the great houses of Britain. It is also one of the few plants that has genuinely caused a huge number of deaths across the world. In Britain, the habit of chewing, smoking and snuffing of tobacco was introduced by sailors and traders to the main ports, and slowly spread across the country. If you live in an older property, you may often find broken pieces of white clay pipes in your garden, the smaller the pipe bowl the older the pipe, because as the tax on tobacco decreased, the size of the bowls increased as tobacco became cheaper to buy. The wealthier classes often preferred to take a pinch of snuff, rather than smoke, and the taking of snuff cleared the head of ill-humours. Very decorative boxes were produced for both men and women, to hold the snuff, which often mixed to their own recipe. Snuff taking must have caused some disruption in churches, as in 1624 Pope Urban VIII felt that it was necessary to publish a decree of excommunication against all those who took snuff in church.

It was soon realised that pests could be killed using tobacco plants. A Victorian garden book, *The Gardener's Assistant*, gave full instructions for growing and processing tobacco for use in the garden to kill aphids and other pests. The shredded leaves were placed in small heaps on the floor. The gardener would then light the leaves and leave them to smoulder in the sealed greenhouse. It was common practise to light the tobacco at night and leave the greenhouse sealed until the morning when, by the time the doors were opened, every creepy crawly would be dead. It was certainly the practice of later gardeners, if not the earlier ones, to take a deep breath and then light the tobacco by starting at the furthest point and working back towards the door. Tobacco paper could be bought to make what was effectively a smoke producing-firework and vaporisers could also be used. A copper dish would be filled with liquid nicotine and then placed on a small burner that vaporised the liquid nicotine, rather like the burners used for vapouring essential oil to scent the house, allowing the lethal fumes to fill the glasshouse. During earlier periods nicotine was being commercially extracted from the tobacco waste of the cigarette industry. Nicotine was so powerful that only six ounces were mixed with a hundred gallons of water to make a spray. Soap was often added to the water as it washes off the protective film of the aphids to increase the killing efficiency of the nicotine mixture. A soapy water mixture sprayed onto aphids will actually kill them without the need of any nicotine at all. Nicotine powder could be applied as a powder using a shaker, often the sort used by cooks for flour; or by puffing it onto the plants using a small pair of bellows. The bellows are about 30cm long and were originally used by the upper classes to powder their wigs to kill lice and enrich the colour. Gardeners, who are always adapting things for use in the garden, began to use the bellows for spraying plants with powders. During the Victorian era, the bellows were manufactured specifically for gardeners, with different shaped ends available to give a more efficient delivery of the powder.

My first Saturday Garden Boy job was for an old man who had worked at The Royal Botanical Gardens at Kew. He told me how he and his colleagues would save all their old cigarette butts and boil them in a barrel of water outdoors. The liquid was sprayed on plants to kill greenfly and other pests. It is now illegal in the UK to kill greenfly with nicotine; but if you want to kill yourself, the government are quite happy for you to do so.

It would seem that not everybody approved of tobacco, for no less a person than king James 1 of England, VI of Scotland, certainly did not approve and was centuries ahead of his time with his views of the negative properties of tobacco. He wrote a pamphlet, *A Counterblast to Tobacco*, which was a scathing on the new fashion and the evils of tobacco, calling it:

> 'A custom loathsome to the eye, hateful to the nose, harmful to the brain, dangerous to the lungs, and in the black stinking fume thereof nearest resembling the horrible stygian smoke of the pit that is bottomless.'

James used analogy and the current medical theory to make his case. He was not averse to moralising either. This is not a pamphlet for the politically correct. Having first made a racial attack against the Indians, whom he blamed for the habit; not only did they smoke tobacco, but it was their cure for the pox! He used the theory of the four humours to explain the damage that smoking causes. Sadly, it would take several centuries before medical science agreed with him.

Taylor studied the effects of tobacco and decided that whether it was smoked, chewed or taken as snuff, that it was dangerous to the health. He said that in 1847 a man was charged with trying to kill his wife by adding snuff to her ale. She had her stomach pumped very soon after drinking the mixture and survived. An expert medical witness said that a mere quarter of an ounce would be enough to kill three people. The case was dropped because there was not enough proof of criminal intent to murder.

But the experts often disagreed. Brook quoted the following observations made by Dr Cullen, who disapproved of tobacco and had said:

> 'Tobacco is a well-known plant of a narcotic quality which it discovers in all persons even in small quantaties when first applied to them. I have known a small quantity when first Snuffed up the nose produce

stupor, vomiting, etc., and large quantities to produce death.'

Which he followed with his own observation that although Dr Cullen had decided that tobacco and snuff are dangerous, people continued to '... snuff, smoke and chew for a life time without receiving the slightest injury!'

To further enhance his case, Brook, who was obviously a user of tobacco, tells the tale of the Persian King, Xerxes, who offered a reward to anyone who could invent a new pleasure for him. Brook remarked that:

'If some one could have taught his majesty to smoke, he would undoubtedly have received the reward. For there is indeed a pleasure in smoking (especially if the smoker has been a while without the accustomed pipe) which none but the smoker can understand, and few describe.'

Which shows how medical ideas can change over time.

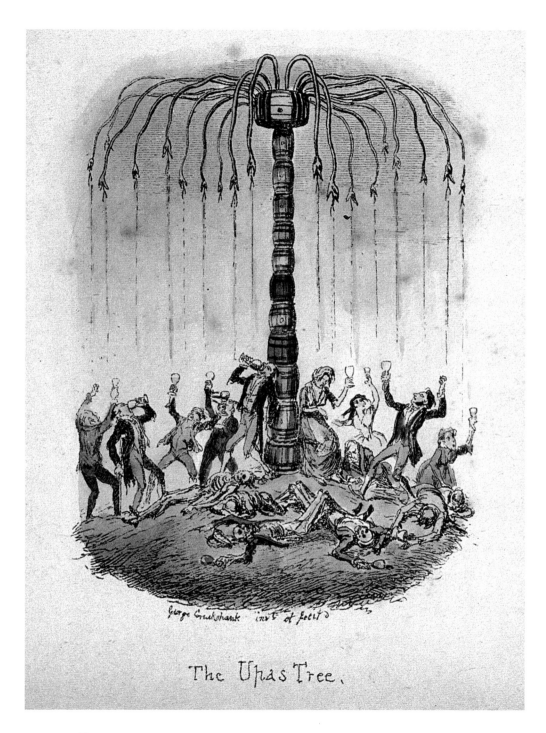

The Upas Tree.

UPAS TREE

The upas tree has acquired a wealth of myth over the centuries, but is not a tree that can be easily grown in Britain. The tree has many practical uses, providing shade in the hot climate of its native lands and for its wood; but it is mostly renowned for the poison that is derived from it, which was used to poison the heads of arrows, blow-pipe darts and spears. The name is from the Javanese for poison.

Genus: *Antiaris*
Species: *toxicaria*
Family: Moraceae
Common Names:
Upas Tree.
Poison Tree.
Deciduous Tree
Active Constituents:
Cardenolide
glycosides.

The tree had a reputation for being the most poisonous in the world and tales of it eventually became so outlandish, that many believed that the tree was in fact a complete fabrication. Erasmus Darwin translated a description of the tree that had been written by the Dutch surgeon N.P. Foersch, although it now seems that the author was John Nicols Foersch, who had been stationed in Java. Foersch blamed the naturalists, who, writing for dramatic effect, also made the upas tree appear to be too deadly and marvellous to be a reality.

Foersch claimed that in 1774 he was working for the Dutch East-India Company where he had heard stories of a tree that the local Javanese called *Bohun-Upas*, and of the powerful poison that it was said to produce. He says that he himself was dubious of the existence of the tree, but determined to discover the truth for himself and only rely on his personal observations. He obtained a pass from the Governor-General and a recommendation from a Malaysian priest to another priest who lived about fifteen miles from the tree. This priest had been appointed by the Emperor to tend to the spiritual and bodily needs of convicts who had been condemned to death, and whose sentence was to go to the tree to collect the poison, from which the Emperor derived a great income. Foersch said that the upas tree was encircled by hills and mountains and that nothing grew within twelve miles of the tree; not a tree, shrub, nor even a blade of grass. No animals lived there and even the birds avoided flying close by. The cause of this was thought to be a lethal gas that the tree continually emitted. The condemned men were sent to the priest for instruction on how to harvest the poison. They were told to approach the tree when the wind blew from behind them and to make the journey as quickly as possible before the wind changed direction. If they survived and returned with the poison their lives wold be spared, so there was a good incentive. Before leaving the priest's house, the convict would be given a leather hood that covered their head and reached down to the chest. Eye holes were cut into the leather and covered with glass. The man was also given a pair of leather gloves and a silver or tortoiseshell box into which he was to place any poison that he was able to collect. The man was permitted to say farewell to his family and friends then, after prayers for his safety, he was escorted for two miles before he was abandoned to continue on his own in search of the deadly tree. Foersch claimed to have seen a list of over seven hundred criminals who had received and carried out the sentence, out of which he said that only two in twenty ever returned. Foersch said he was present at Soura-Charta in February 1776, when thirteen of the emperor's concubines were convicted of infidelity and sentenced to death. Thirteen posts, each about five feet high had been set out. Having kissed the Koran, the victims were tied to the posts and their breasts stripped bare. They remained like this for some time, attended to by priests, as prayers were said for the women. The judge eventually made a signal, upon which the executioner took a lancet that was similar to the fleam that was commonly used to bleed horses, except that this lancet had been poisoned using some upas gum. The executioner went to each woman in turn and made a cut on the middle of her breast. Within five minutes the women began to tremble with involuntary muscle spasms. They cried out to Mahomet for mercy as they suffered great agony. Poersch noted from his watch, that within sixteen minutes all of the thirteen women were dead. Foersch claimed that he had witnessed more human executions and later he had carried out experiments with the poison on animals. He repeated the method used in the executions that he witnessed and also administered the drug orally. All the animal victims died quickly, within minutes.

Foersch wrote that the local men of 'fashion and quality' carried knives poisoned with upas and that many locals and Europeans died as a result of the poison, sometimes from the cut of a bladed weapon, and other times from poisoned food and drink. The Dutch were alleged to have suffered great losses of soldiers when the Malaysians poisoned the water supplies during military conflicts. Learning from their experience, the Dutch henceforth only drank the water after testing it by releasing fish and observing whether they lived; or not.

The noxious fumes may have been explained by Sykes in 1837, when he suggested that volcanic gasses may have been responsible for some of the barrenness of the area; whilst if a tree produced a lot of shade, very little would grow beneath it. Rick J Willis in his book, *The History of Allelopathy*, suggested that Foersch was preparing to publish a book on the East Indies, and in a good example of self-publicity, had embellished his account to create interest in his forthcoming book, and hopefully help to sell more copies.

Although the upas tree may not live up to its terrible reputation, there are examples of plants that do in fact secrete chemicals from their roots that are toxic, not only to other species of plants, but even their own, to reduce the competition for space, water, light and nutrients. This is called allelopathy. Scientists from the University of Delaware carried out research that discovered that the reed *Phragmites australis* secretes an acid that breaks down the structural protein and so destroys the roots of other species so that they can grow in their place. The plant is actively removing opposition to make space for its own expansion, whereas most other plants only discourage the germination and growth of other species. Many old gardening books do not include walnut trees in orchards, but suggest they are planted elsewhere because of their supposed effect on people. Ferns, garlic mustard, pine trees, juniper and sunflowers use allelopathy to reduce the competition from other species that are growing in their habitats Rhododendrons are commonly said to poison the soil around them, but this has not yet been scientifically proven, although there is little doubt that the dense evergreen shade they produce does reduce the number of other species. Yew trees also produce dense shade when allowed to grow naturally, but they also secrete chemicals to inhibit the germination and growth of other species. Research is being carried out to discover whether the chemicals produced by some plants could be put to practical use as weed killers.

The eucalyptus tree, in a manner that is similar to the mythical deathly gas given off by the upas tree, really does give off volatile oils from its leaves, especially in very hot weather. The oils fall onto the soil where they negatively affect the germination of seeds and the growth of roots and shoots of surface rooting plants. Plants can kill other plants, not just humans!

WHITE BRYONY

White Bryony is the only member of the cucumber family that is native to Britain, but is not often found in the north of England and Scotland. It is a common woodland and hedgerow plant, with vine-like leaves and green/white flowers that are followed by dull, red berries. During the autumn, the stems of the plant disappear, leaving little bunches of berries hanging in the hedges. The root can be very long and thick, as much thirty centimetres

Genus: *Brionica*
Species: *dioica*
Family: Cucurbitaceae
Common Names:
 White Bryony.
 Mandrake.
 Devil's Turnip.
Herbaceous Perennial
Active Constituents:
 Bryonicine.
 Bryonidin.

or longer and eight to ten centimetres thick at the widest part.

It is this root that the herbalist Gerard said that 'idle drones' who have nothing to do with their time other than to eat and drink, carved the white bryony root into the shape of men and women, and then sold it as a real mandrake to gullible customers; undoubtedly at the high price of a real mandrake root. Matthiolus added a refinement, where the maker of fake mandrakes would insert barley or millet seeds where there should be body hair before replanting the briony roots. When the grains had sprouted, the root was dug up and the fresh sprouts trimmed with a sharp knife so they would appear to be head hair, beards or any other bodily hair.

The Germanic goddess, *Alraunwurzel*, was represented in many households by having an *Alruna*, a carved wooden mannikin. A carved mandrake root was the best choice, but growing a mandrake root to a size suitable for carving was probably difficult in Germany, so it is likely that they also used white bryony instead. William Coles said that witches would use mandrake roots, or white bryony, to make images of the person on whom they wished to exercise their magic.

Selling a white bryony root as a real mandrake was a Tudor con trick, but not quite so much as may be expected. I have led numerous tours at the medieval gardens where there is a poisonous plants garden that includes white bryony. On seeing the plant, some men who used to lead plough horses have pointed and said, 'That's mandrake!' They then went on to explain that they used to keep a bryony root in their pockets during the ploughing season. If a horse went lame they would cut off a piece of root and feed it to the horse as a pain killer so that it could continue to work. So not quite the con trick that it may have at first appeared.

John Arderne gave a bryony recipe to cure cramp or spasms; the root should be boiled in water and then crushed in linseed oil, lily oil or chamomile oil and used as plaster on the affected part of the body. He also mentions the plant as one of the ingredients of a potion used by crooks to send the unwary to sleep before robbing them. Another medicinal use of the root was as a violent purge, but it was always a risky option, as were other violent purges, which in modern times are certainly not recommended for use.

There are recipes for bryony water, a medicine to aid birth, remove afterbirth, a dead foetus or to induce and abortion. Besides 12 pounds of white Bryony root the recipe included well know abortifacients such as savin and pennyroyal, as well as rue and castor (probably *Ricinus*). The roots of white bryony could be bruised and applied to the body where there were broken bones to draw out the splinters. It would do the same for arrowheads, splinters and thorns. If wine was added it could be used to break boils and whitlows.

The *Trotula* included a recipe to add a touch of red to a pale face. The bryony was washed, chopped finely and left to dry. The root was then crushed into a powder and finally mixed with rose water. A cotton or fine linen cloth was used to put the mixture on the face, and voila! the cheeks would become red as if it were the natural colouring of the woman's cheek.

WOODY NIGHTSHADE

As mentioned before, many people mistake this plant for deadly nightshade and there are many instances of this happening both online and in magazine articles. Woody nightshade grows in hedges, on banks and waste land. It is a climbing plant that twines around its supports, with attractive mauve flowers which have a yellow protruding centre, which is actually a cluster of stamens.

If bruised all parts of the plant give off a rather sickly scent that sticks to your hands, but the smell disappears when the stems are dried. The berries work their way through the sequence of traffic lights, beginning green, changing to a yellowy orange, before finally becoming a bright red. The berries are most poisonous before they ripen. Gerard poetically described the berries as being like burnished coral. He

Genus: *Solanum*
Species: *dulcamara*
Family: Solanaceae
Common Names:
  Woody Nightshade.
  Bittersweet.
  Felenwood.
  Granny's Nightcap.
  Dulcamara.
  Amara dulcis.
Herbaceous Perennial
Active Constituents:
  Solanine.
  Dulcamarine.

finally added a cynical remark concerning the many names given by various writers, 'But every author must for his credit say something, although but to small purpose.'

The bittersweet name was first recorded by Turner who simply anglicised the Latin name of, *Amara dulcis*. The name bittersweet refers to the fact that if the root or stem are chewed the initial taste is of bitterness, soon followed by that of sweetness which comes from the dulcamarine. I have not tried this for myself as I find the smell of the plant too sickly to even want to taste it.

Although it is a member of the same *Solanaceae* plant family as deadly nightshade, woody nightshade does not have the dilating effect on people's eyes. Gerard thought that the juice of the plant would dissolve congealed blood, making it a good treatment for those who had become bruised through falling from high places. It was said to avert the effects of the Evil Eye, so shepherds and those who looked after cattle, horses and pigs would tie bittersweet around the necks of their animals as a protection against witchcraft and magic. Culpepper says that this would work on humans too. The plant is also notable as being the first one that Culpepper deals with in his herbal, where he still called it *Amara Dulcis*. After writing a few lines about how the herb is useful for the liver and spleen, breathing problems, dropsy, yellow and black bile, jaundice and women newly brought to bed, meaning that they are in the later stages of pregnancy, Culpepper appears to suffer from an unusual moment of self-doubt because he then added:

> 'They that think the use of these medicines is too brief, it is only for the cheapness of the book; let them read those books of mine, of the last edition, viz. Reverius, Veslingus, Riolanus, Johnson, Sennertus, and Physic for the Poor.'

The plant was part of the British Pharmacopeia until 1907, being used for its mild narcotic properties. Other uses included asthma, chronic bronchial catarrh and whooping cough; and for skin problems such as ulcers, scrofula and for kidney problems.

If you like the flowers but find he plant too spindly for growing in the garden, grow *Solanum crispum*, the variety 'Glasnevin' is the best for purple flowers. For white flowers, try *Solanum jasminoides*, but both can become unruly if not kept under control. If you want to grow it up arbours and pergolas, train the stems around the uprights as a spiral. This will encourage flowering shoots all the way up the stem, rather than just at the top, where it has a habit over growing rather over-enthusiastically. I have also pruned and trained it as a free-standing shrub.

banned in Switzerland. A similar ban spread to most of Europe, but not in Portugal, Spain or Britain.

As with many fashionable drugs, absinthe acquired its own rituals in preparation for drinking. Wormwood is very bitter; hence one of its traditional uses to stimulate appetite. The drink would be poured to fill the bottom rounded part of a glass, a special spoon with decorative piercings would be placed on top of the glass, onto which a sugar lump was placed; then iced water would be poured onto the sugar lump. The absinthe would then develop the louche, by changing colour to a milky white.

Recent research suggests that the original absinthe may not be as bad as once thought; possibly, no worse for you than any other extremely strong spirit. Wormwood was no longer believed to be the cause of the absinthe madness, but in the United States of America, they are not so sure, and wormwood is a banned ingredient for anything intended for human consumption.

Genus: Taxus
Species: *baccata*
Family: Taxaceae
Common Names:
 Yew
Evergreen Tree
Active Constituents:
 Taxane alkaloids

YEW

Yew prefers dry shade, is a slow growing tree that can reach heights of 20m or more, but it rarely grows straight upright in Britain. The leaves are dark green, looking very similar to rosemary, as Thomas Hanmer noted. He suggested that yew was as worthy of a place in a garden as any of the exotic evergreens that were available, and that it is best grown from berries rather than transplanted because the transplanted specimens rarely thrived. The *baccata* part of the name means bearing red berries, but in fact the berries are botanically, arils, modified cones, containing a single seed. In spring, clouds of pollen can often be seen falling from the branches which can be a problem for people with some allergies.

Yew trees can live for a very long time, developing enormous trunks and an air of ancient mysticism. The leaves are poisonous to most livestock, and it is sensible not to grow yew where animals can graze on it; except for deer, who can happily eat the leaves without ill-effect. I once visited a garden where the yew hedge had been kept neatly cut as far up as the deer could reach to graze on the leaves. The ancient Gaulish king, Catuvolcus, who tiring of fighting Julius Caesar, was said to have committed suicide with an extract of yew sap.

The berries are poisonous in a way, but not completely so. I have met several older people, usually men, who have told me that as children they often ate the berries, but you have to suck off the soft red outer and then spit out the stone without scratching the surface of the stone. If you examine a yew berry you will notice that the top end is fairly open; placing the berry between your teeth with the top pointing away from your mouth, gently close your jaw. The stone will be ejected and you can then safely swallow the soft part. There is a certain sweetness, but flavour is not particularly wonderful, and the texture is a little odd, so it is best not to even try. Foxes are especially fond of yew berries. If you find a tree where the berries have fallen on the ground, start walking away from the tree. You may find small clusters of stones. This is because when the fox has eaten the berries, stomach acid reacts with the coating on the stone and the fox then vomits, leaving the cluster of seed stones. This is the way that the yew tree ensures it spreads its seeds as far away as possible, so that new seedlings have the space and light to germinate and thrive.

Yew makes an excellent hedge and having fine evergreen leaves it makes a good backdrop to other plants. If the hedge is cut regularly you will also reduce the number of berries that form. Yew has the advantage over some hedging plants, such as leyland cypress in that it can be cut back very hard. Some years ago, at Packwood House where there is some yew topiary known as the Sermon on the Mount and the Twelve Apostles, the National Trust decided that some of the apostles were becoming slightly podgy. So, working on two or three apostles at a time, they simply cut off all of the branches to leave a bare trunk. The yew grew back and once the branches were long enough the topiary was trimmed to shape. If you look at a mature yew tree, you will notice the green shoots growing all over the trunk, which is a good indication that it can withstand hard pruning. Do not be tempted to leave short lengths of stumps as you cut off the branches as they usually die. From practical experience, I have found the biggest danger for the berries is when they fall onto a paved path, when they can easily make you slide or fall over.

Yew had a reputation for being dangerous, and became associated with witchcraft. In the play, *Macbeth*, the second witch called for:

'Gall of goat, and slips of Yew
Sliver'd in the moon's eclipse.'

Everybody knew that yew is poisonous, and it may be the poison, *Hebenon,* that Shakespeare is thinking of in *Hamlet*, as yew is called *ibenbaum* in Dutch and *Ibenboom* in some German regions, whilst Classical texts describe Hebanon as a tree, making it a more likely candidate than hemlock for the poison that Claudius used to kill the elderly king Hamlet;

In another of Shakespeare's plays, *Richard II*, Lord Scroope tells King Richard that:

'Thy very beadsmen bend their bows
Of double-fatal yew against thy State.'

He is referring to the yew as not only being poisonous, but it is also deadly because it was the best wood to make the English longbow that had proved to be such an effective weapon in France, but would now be used during the ensuing civil war, killing the king's own subjects. Yew was the best wood for longbows because the white, outer sap wood of yew is able to withstand stretching, whilst the heartwood can withstand contraction, an ideal combination for a bow wood. It is often said that yew was grown in churchyards to provide wood to make the bows, but although yew branches can be used to make a good bow, the trunk is usually the best wood and the trees would need to be cut down. The finest yew wood for bows must be grown slowly and straight, free of wind twist. Good yew wood became so difficult to obtain that laws were passed to ensure good quality bow staves would be available. In 1472, Edward IV issued a statute that stated that because:

'… great scarcity of bowstaves is now in this realm, and the bowstaves that be in the realm be sold at an excessive price, whereby the exercise of archery is greatly discontinued, and almost lost.'

The statute decreed that for every tun of merchandise brought into the country, there should be four good quality bowstaves and to ensure that the merchants did not buy cheap wood that would be useless to make good bows, inspectors would check the staves to ensure that they were of a suitable quality and then mark the staves. A fine of half a mark, 6s. 8d, was in place for the omission of each stave that was due.

There are many ancient yews in churchyards, but they are probably there as a symbol of eternal life, being one of the few evergreen trees in Britain. There are some fine ancient yews in the churchyard of Pennant Melangell in Wales. The trees would be out of the way of browsing stock animals because most churches were enclosed. Coles recounted a story concerning a certain Master Wells, a minister at Adderbury in Oxfordshire, who saw some boys breaking branches from a yew tree in the churchyard, which upset him so much, that to prevent it happening again he ordered somebody to cut the tree down. The tree was duly felled and the waste placed in Master Wells' back yard. Unfortunately, his cows fed on the branches and within a few hours, two of them died. Coles considered this a just reward. Nicander of Colphon wrote a book in verse, *Counter Poisons*, in which he describes the agonies of a victim of yew poisoning:

'Be quick with aid, when yew tree juice with pains.
With anguish thrilling potion whelms the veins.
The tongue is under-swol'n; the lips protrude
In heavy tumours, with dry froth bedew'd:
The gums are cleft; the heart quick terror shakes
Smit with the bane; the labouring reason quakes.'

The remedy is a purge to empty the stomach.

Yew branches had often been used to represent the palm trees of the bible during Palm Sunday celebrations in England. In 1656 Coles remarked that it is only recently that the old custom of setting garlands in churches has ceased, but that in some parts of the country yew was still used to decorate the churches at Christmas.

The new growth of yew branches can be processed to extract Taxol, an anti-cancer drug, used to treat cancers affecting the uterus and ovaries. The National Trust has many yew hedges, so if the clippings are kept free of rubbish and bagged up, they can provide a good source of income.

Yew wood is particularly good for making furniture. The heartwood has a deep gold colour that may be highlighted by knots and other markings.

PITCHER PLANT

Genus: *Sarracenia*
Species: *flava*
Family: Sarraceniaceae
Common Names:
Pitcher Plant.
Perennial

Some deaths in the garden are caused not by poisoning, but by the plants actively eating their living prey. *Sarracenia* is one of the easiest carnivorous plants to grow and it is now readily available in many British garden centres. For the specialist, there are nurseries that can provide cultivars with a range of different markings and colourings. Carnivorous plants usually grow in acidic sphagnum bogs that are low in nitrogen, so the plant needs to supplement its diet by using insects as a source of food. If the supply of nitrogen increases the plants produce fewer pitchers to catch prey.

Sarracenia will survive outdoors in Britain; the cold is beneficial as they need a period of dormancy over winter to produce flowers. If grown in water, the tops may be frozen and die but new pitchers will rise from the rhizomes in Spring. There are several records of *Sarracenia* being found in the wild in Britain, mostly likely as a result of being deliberately planted, rather than from seed as an escapee from garden plants. The first colony that I heard about was in the Peak District National Park, in Derbyshire, but I have since heard of others in Dorset and Chobham.

The pitcher usually has a cap over the top, the operculum, to prevent rain water getting into the pitcher body and diluting the digestive juices that the plant produces to extract the nutrients from its victims' bodies. The top of the pitcher called the peristome and is the part that produces the nectar to attract the insects. The nectar of *Sarracenia flava* contains coniine, also found in hemlock, which is narcotic to the insects, so having eaten their fill, the insects become quite woozy. The surface of the peristome is very waxy; the drunken insects have difficulty in maintaining a good grip, and slip into the trumpets, which are fluted to encourage a good journey downwards. The nectar is also addictive, so if the insects do survive their first meal, they are compelled to go back for seconds. At the bottom of the pitcher is a pool of liquid that contains the digestive enzymes that break the insect down into the nutrients into a form that the plant can then feed on. The liquid in some species of pitcher plants has an even more complex function than may be expected. Recent research has shown that the liquid has its own eco-system. Midge, mosquito and flesh fly larvae; mites; rotifers; copepods; nematodes and multicellular algae all live and thrive in the liquid. When the prey falls into the pitcher the midge larvae shred it into smaller pieces, then bacteria eat the shredded pieces and the rotifers eat the bacteria, and eventually the pitcher plant absorbs the waste produced by the rotifers. The sides of the trumpets are often very smooth to prevent the insects climbing out and one Venezuelan species, *Heliamphora nutans*, has downward facing hairs which hold water droplets, preventing the ants, their main prey, from keeping their grip; the ants then aquaplane to their doom. Some *Nepenthes* pitcher plants from Borneo are even able to turn off their traps for part of the day to enable the scouting ants to return safely to their nests and then send even more ants to the plant. *Nepenthes lowii* has two types of pitchers. Some grow at ground level, but the second type are produced high in the trees. Video film shows that the montane tree shrew, *Tupaia montana*, eats the nectar that the plant produces, and then defecates into the pitcher, the faeces being rich in nitrogen feed the plant. Such symbiosis may have led to tales of the large *Nepenthes rajah* of Borneo devouring small rodents. This may occur accidentally at times, but it is not the plant's intention. Even more unusual is that Nepenthes hemsleyanais used by woolly bats as a daytime roost, even though other suitable roosting sites are available elsewhere in the woodland. The plant benefits as the bats faeces provide nearly a third of the plant's nitrogen. The bats are provided with a secure hideout, and the humid atmosphere in the pitcher helps them to avoid dehydration.

SUNDEW

The sundew is a carnivorous plant that is native to Britain. The genus name, *Drosera* comes from, *drosos,* the Greek for dew or dewdrops. The earlier Latin name of *Ros solis*, means dew of the sun that led to the common English name of sundew. It grows on the boggy heath, marshland and peatland areas in Britain. It can be found in the South West and North West of England and in many areas of Northern Ireland, Scotland and

Genus: *Drosera*
Species: *rotundifolia*
Family: Droseraceae
Other Names:
  Sundew.
  Rosa solis.
  Fly Catcher.
  Youthwort.
  Lust Wort.
Hardy Perennial

Wales. I have seen it growing in the boggy area not far from Corfe Castle. It is small plant, only growing to 5cm in diameter, and forms a rosette of leaves. The leaves have red hairs that secrete a sweet, sticky mucilage that has the appearance of dewdrops, which attract insects which land and then become stuck. As the insect struggles, the hairs bend towards the centre of the leaf to cover the insect as much as possible. The insect can take as long as fifteen minutes to die; death usually coming from the result of exhaustion after struggling to escape, or from asphyxiation caused by the sticky mucilage blocking the spiracles which the insect uses to breathe. The plant then secretes enzymes that break down the insect so the plant can absorb the nutrients. It can take several hours, or up to a day, for the prey to be devoured. The plant will not secrete the enzymes if an inorganic object becomes caught on the leaves.

The roots of the plant are short and fibrous. They do not need to be large as they are not needed to provide nutrients, only to hold the plant in position. Sundews produce insect pollinated flowers, so the flowers stems are held above the leaves. It was originally thought that this was to avoid the pollinating insects being trapped, but research now shows that the insects that pollinate the flowers are not the same types that usually get trapped. The flowers open in direct sunlight and face towards the sun throughout the day.

Gerard noted that the leaves had, 'dew on them even when the sun shineth hottest, even at high noone'. He said that if the water of the plant was distilled in a glass, the liquid will have a glittering yellow colour, like gold, and if silver was placed into the water, it too would be coloured like gold. How good was the gold colouring? Would it be good enough to fool somebody into thinking that the silver was really gold? Another comment was that if female cattle ate the plant, the effect was that it 'stirreth up a desire to lust, which were before was dulled, and, as it were asleepe.'

Another problem Gerard mentioned is that the plant was blamed for causing liver damage to the sheep that grazed on it, leading to sundew being nicknamed Red Rot. Another plant said to cause similar liver damage was the marsh pennywort, *Hydrocotyle vulgaris*, which was also known as White Rot. Gerard said that the common people made a liqueur, *Rosa Solis*, by distilling the sundew leaves in wine. In later periods, it was usually made by steeping the leaves in a spirit alcohol. The drink was said to have the property of maintaining youthfulness and to be an aphrodisiac. Gerard thoughtfully provided a recipe for those who were tempted to test the drink's reputation:

'Steep Sundew leaves in spirits of wine i.e. brandy. Add cinnamon, cloves, mace, ginger, nutmeg, sugar and a few grains of musk. Stand the mix in a sealed glass for ten days or more in a sunny position. Strain, bottle and keep it for your use.'

Both Gerard and Culpepper said that the juice placed on the skin produced blisters and that because of this, some physicians thought that the plant should not be used internally, but as sundew was commonly used for coughs and other bronchial problems, this fear seems to have mostly been ignored.

On the Isle of Man, the sticky leaves could be slipped into the clothing of a would-be lover; the leaves being used as a form of sympathetic magic to stick you together. The more practically minded Highland Scots used the roots to produce a purple dye, and a yellow dye by processing the whole plant with ammonia.

Modern herbal and homeopathic medicines use sundew for whooping cough, asthma and bronchitis, with the juice being used for verrucas and warts. Current research shows that extracts from *Drosera rotundifolia* have good anti-inflammatory and antispasmodic effects.

VENUS FLYTRAP

T he Venus flytrap is the most well-known of the carnivorous plants, being instantly recognisable to just about everybody. The species name *muscipula* is Latin for a mouse trap, which is an accurate description of the plants jaws, although the Venus flytrap is a small plant that can only catch insects, not small rodents. As with other carnivorous plants, the Venus flytrap naturally lives in areas of soil that contains little nutrition, so it needs to catch insects to obtain the necessary nutrients to survive. It is native

Genus: *Dionaea*
Species: *muscipula*
Family: Droseraceae
Common Name:
  Venus Flytrap.
Tender Perennial

to subtropical wetlands on the East Coast of the United States of America in North and South Carolina. The traps are formed at the end of the leaves. The inside of the jaw can be red or have a pink flush, and there is nectar on jaws to entice the victim. There are hairs on the jaws that must be hit twice in twenty seconds before the jaws will close, in one tenth of a second. If the prey is too small to be worth the energy expended to digest it the jaws will remain slightly open to allow it to escape, and the jaw will usually open again in twelve hours.

If the prey is of a suitable size, the jaws will seal tightly to prevent the victim escaping. Five more movements need to be detected by the plant before it begins producing the enzymes that will digest the insect, when the jaws form a tight seal and effectively become a stomach. Each trap can only capture prey three times before it dies. I used to teach Horticulture at a college where there was a small collection of carnivorous plants. We asked the students not to touch the Venus Flytraps, but the younger students couldn't resist the temptation and kept knocking the hairs and the poor plants eventually died from expending too much energy for food that that they never received.

Arthur Dobbs, Governor of North Carolina, is credited with being the first person to scientifically describe the plant, in 1763. He named it the Fly Trap Sensitive. It was the first plant to be botanically described as a carnivorous plant. The plant was certainly known in England by 1765, because a dried sample had been sent to John Ellis of London by Mr John Bartram of Philadelphia, the King's botanist. Ellis was a linen merchant, but he was also a notable naturalist. He was a member of the Royal Society of London and that of Uppsala, and was in contact with other naturalists by letter.

In 1770, he published a short book of only twenty-six pages titled, *Directions for bringing over Seeds and Plants from the East-Indies and other Distant Countries, in a State of Vegetation,* with a section at the end concerning the Venus Flytrap. He included a copy of a letter that he had sent to friend Charles Linnaeus, dated 23 September 1769, in which he says how with the assistance of Dr Solander, he dissected the dried plant material. They decided that the plant was related to *Drosera*, also known as Rosa solis, a carnivorous plant that grew in England, commonly known as the Sundew; but as they only had a dried specimen, they failed to realise that the plant they had dissected was also carnivorous. Luckily another botanist, Mr. William Young, also of Philadelphia, had collected more plants and managed to transport them alive back to England, with a description of their native habitat. Ellis writes of the plant that:

'It is now likely to become an inhabitant of the curious gardens in this country, and merits the attention of the ingenious.'

Ellis included a complete botanical description of the plant, which he had named Venus's Fly Trap. He noted that he knows that Linnaeus has seen Mimosa, the Sensitive Plant, but that the plant he is going to describe is even more exciting. With his original letter, he had sent some dried specimens of the leaves and flowers and a full colour painting. Beneath the picture, Ellis described the white flowers as being similar to the English wild flower, lady's smock, *Cardamine pratense*. He then gave a description of the trap mechanism:

> 'Each leaf is a miniature figure of a rat trap with teeth; closing on every fly or other insect that creeps between its lobes, and squeezes it to death.'

In the main text, Ellis mentioned the nectar used to lure the prey and how the jaws would close and squeeze the victim to death and that they remained closed until the insect has been devoured. He carried out experiments with pieces of straw and noticed that the plant could not discern whether its prey was a living creature or not, because the trap would still close.

Growing the plant was experimental for Ellis. He knew that the plant needed a moist soil and shade, but he was unsure how much cold the plant could withstand, and he certainly did not know that it needed a period of dormancy in order to achieve its full life expectancy of twenty to thirty years. He had kept plants alive beneath bell jars, covering them with straw during very cold weather. He had also discovered the plant becomes more active with heat, so he suggested keeping them in pots, standing in dishes of water and keeping them in a ventilated stove house.

Despite the proof that both sundew and the Venus Flytrap were carnivorous, Erasmus Darwin believed that the plants killed the insects to protect themselves from being eaten.

It is now very easy to buy a Venus Flytrap plant from most of the larger garden centres in Britain because micropropagation has made it easy for them to be mass-produced and affordable. Plant breeders have now produced many different cultivars of the plant for the serious collector. This is very much a good thing as collecting of plants from the wild has become a major problem. In 2014, the state of North Carolina passed legislation to classify the theft of naturally growing Venus flytraps in some counties as a crime and by 2015 it was thought that there may have only been 33,000 plants still surviving in the wild. The Venus flytrap can be grown from seed, which is readily available, but you will need to be patient as it will take up to five years for the plants to become mature. Some growers recommend removing the flowering stalks so the plant will put its energy into producing more of the traps.

There are claims that an extract from the Venus flytrap can be used as a remedy for Crohn's Disease, HIV and skin cancer, although medical research has so far failed to prove the claims.

GROWING POISONOUS PLANTS

Nearly all the plants mentioned in this book can be grown perfectly legally, some may already be growing in your garden, but obviously, cannabis and any other plants that are illegal in your part of the world should be avoided. I would also be wary of growing deadly nightshade in built-up areas where there are lots of children as the seeds are easily spread by birds and many people do not recognise the plant or how dangerous it can be.

Most of the plants in this book grow naturally in the wild in Britain. Some of the less hardy plants will survive a British summer if the seeds are sown indoors and the plants slowly exposed to the outdoor conditions once the risk of frost has passed. It is always best to give a plant the conditions that it prefers in the wild, but many plants are surprisingly adaptable.

Some tender plants can survive winter under cover and are best grown in pots so they can be easily moved. The annuals will die at the end of the year and set seed, so allow seed to develop and ripen if you want to grow the plant the following year. It is usually best to allow the seed cases of herbaceous and annuals to begin to dry and then cut the stems before the seed ripens and falls out. Paper bags can be tied over the seed heads and the stems hung upside down and allowed to ripen and dry. The seed cases of some plants, such as thorn apple, can have sharp spikes that will easily pierce gloves. From experience, I have learned to put the dried seed cases in a thick plastic bag and then to lightly hit them with a hammer to release the seeds. Seeds should be labelled and stored in paper bags, not plastic, and kept in dry cool conditions. Some seed is best sown when it is fresh and most is best sown within a year although some seeds will remain viable for several years or more. In the past, I have failed to label some of my seeds in the mistaken belief that I would remember what they are; it is very easy to forget.

Some seeds may need a period of cold before they will germinate. This can be carried out simply by sowing the seed in trays and leaving the seed trays outside over winter, but make sure the compost will not become water-logged. Another method is to place the seed tray in a plastic bag. Squash out most of the air and seal the bag. Place the bag in a fridge for two weeks. Information for the germination of most seeds can now be found online. A reputable seed company will usually include additional germination requirements on its web site or in a catalogue.

Some seeds may require soaking in water before they are sown, and seeds with hard coatings may need the case thinning by rubbing it carefully with sandpaper to speed the germination process.

When sowing seeds use a good seed compost. Check the compost before buying it if possible. I have lost many seeds and plants that rotted due to composts that retain too much moisture. I usually add some sharp sand to any organic compost that I use for sowing seeds. To sow seeds, fill your seed tray by dropping a large handful of compost in each corner and then fill the middle of the tray so that it is over-flowing. Use a straight piece of wood dragged over the edges of the tray to remove the surplus compost. Lightly tap the seed tray on a firm surface to allow thee compost to settle and then water the seed tray using a watering can with a fine rose or stand the tray in shallow water and allow the water to soak into the compost. Sow your seeds thinly. You may have lots of seeds but you will only need a few plants. Sowing thinly allows space for the seedlings to grow; reduces the chance of disease and makes it easier to remove the individual seedlings when potting on. If seeds have a very long germination period, it is usually best to place the seed tray in a plastic bag, seal the opening and then place the bag somewhere safe and warm where it will not be disturbed. The compost should remain moist in the bag. I have grown quite a few plants using this method; but don't forget to check whether the seeds are shooting.

If you want your plants to remain true to type, especially for named varieties, then the plants must be grown from cuttings to produce clones, as growing from the seed will usually produce genetic variations in the off-spring. If you want to grow your own cultivars, sow the seeds; you can never be certain what you may get, which is half the fun of growing plants from seed.

Soil-based compost, usually marked as loam compost, is best for long-term planting in pots. I always mix general peat, or peat-free based potting compost 50:50 with soil based compost as it is easier to re-wet the compost if it has been allowed to become completely dry during hot or windy weather. The heavier compost also helps to prevent the pot blowing over in the wind. I also place a large stone or a brick in the base of large plastic pots to give them more stability to prevent them blowing over in strong winds.

Many herbaceous plants can be grown from cuttings, especially from the young shoots as they grow in the spring, or as semi-ripe cuttings. To take cuttings in the spring, remove the top 5cm. of the shoot and plant it in a pot with a compost of 50:50 organic compost and sharp sand or perlite. Water the pot using a watering can with a fine rose and put the pot in a warm, light, well-ventilated position. You can use a heated propagator to encourage the roots to develop, or put the pot in a transparent plastic bag, put some short pieces of cane into the pot to stop the bag touching the cutting and then seal the bag. This will prevent the pot drying out, but check that the inside of the bag does not become covered in large droplets of water. Remove the drops as necessary.

To make cuttings from woody plants, a semi ripe cutting taken in late summer is a good method. Remove the new growth that has been produced over the summer using sharp secateurs, keep the cuttings in a plastic bag as you collect them as they can dry very quickly. Prepare a compost of 50:50 organic compost and sharp sand or perlite, put in the pots to below the surface and gently tap the pot on a hard surface to settle the compost. Cut the plant material into pieces about 10cm to 15cm long, cutting the lower end just below a node. Remove the top tip of the cutting, and remove some of the lower leaves. Some people dip the lower end in a hormone rooting powder, I never do as the cuttings will usually grow without any extra help. Insert the cuttings into the compost so that they are stable, but the leaves are not touching the compost, then lightly water and allow any surplus water to drain. You can cover the pots with plastic bags, as described above. Place the pots somewhere warm and light. Remove any fallen leaves or those that are looking diseased.

Herbaceous plants with large fleshy roots or tap roots can usually be grown from root cuttings when the plants are dormant, during mid to late autumn and early winter. They need very little care until they have grown enough to pot on. Only take a third of the parent plant's roots. Note that if the parent plant is variegated, root cuttings will produce offspring with green leaves. Cut pieces of root into 5cm to 10cm lengths. Remove any side rootlets and don't use very thin sections. As you take each cutting, make a slanting cut on the lower end and a horizontal cut at the top; it is very easy to forget which end is the top. Fill your pots with a mix of 50:50 organic compost and sharp sand or perlite. Use a small stick to make a hole and push the root into the compost so that the top of the root is just below the surface. Put an extra 1cm of compost over the cuttings and then cover the compost with a thin layer of horticultural grit. Water the pot using a watering can with a fine rose; you only need a little water. Put the pots in a cold frame if you have one, or stand in a sheltered part of the garden. Once the plants produce shoots, make sure the compost does not dry out completely.

WHAT TO DO IF AFFECTED BY A POISONOUS PLANT

The chances of accidental poisoning are unlikely for adults, but children often chew berries or leaves without knowing the dangers. Most of the risks of poisoning by plants for adults are likely to be from incorrectly identifying wild food-plants when out foraging.

In the event that somebody has eaten part of a poisonous plant take them straight to hospital. If you can, take a sample of the plant that may be used to identify the plant, including leaves, flower, stem and berries with you. If you are not sure which plant caused the problem, take samples of anything that may have caused the problem. The chances are that somebody at Accident and Emergency will recognise the plant, and if not, a specialist probably will. The NHS has a web site, Plant dangers in the Garden and Countryside, which can be found at **http://www.nhs.uk/ Livewell/bites-and-stings/Pages/Plant-dangers-garden-countryside. aspx**. The Royal Horticultural Society have a web page listing potentially dangerous plants: **https://www.rhs.org.uk/advice/profile?pid=524**

If the patient has eaten something, do not try to make them sick. Many old books give recipes for drinks in cases of poisoning, but it is best that you do not give the patient anything other than water.

If an irritant sap gets on the skin, wash it off with soapy water. If symptoms persist, or get worse, take plant samples with you and get the patient to hospital.

Some plant leaves can cause a rash. If this is from irritant hairs on the leaf surface it is unlikely to cause a long-term problem. If you know somebody has been in contact with giant hogweed or rue on a hot sunny day it is best to seek medical advice as soon as possible.

If there is sap or part of the plant in the eyes, wash the eyes with clear water for fifteen minutes. Do not use eyewash. If symptoms persist or get worse or you are still concerned, take plant samples with you and take the patient to hospital.

Many areas in the UK have drop-in medical centres, but they may not be prepared for poisoning cases. Phone them first to make sure before going there, as it may be better to go straight to hospital.

OTHER POISONOUS PLANTS

There are many plants that can have an adverse effect on people. In some cases, it may be pollen, which can cause problems such as hay fever. Some trees use the wind for pollination, so clouds of pollen can fill the air, as there is less chance for pollen to land on the correct flower than with insect pollination. Most grasses are also pollinated by using the wind. Open flowers, like the daisy family, produce lots of pollen. Garden cultivars usually have more petals, so less pollen. This is good for those with allergies, but not for the insects who feed on the flowers.

Some plants have hairy leaves and stems that rub on the skin and damage the surface leaving red marks and causing itching for hours or even days. This is usually an abrasive action, rather than an allergic one.

Plants grow thorns to defend themselves from herbivores that want to eat them; but also against gardeners with secateurs, who want to prune them. Wear good gloves and be careful of your eyes. I know professional gardeners who wear eye protection when pruning lots of thorn-laden plants. Some thorns such as pyracantha and blackthorn sting and go septic very quickly in the skin. Rose thorns can lead to tetanus, so make sure you are up to date with your course of tetanus injections.

If you know that the tiny hairs that some plants have will affect your breathing, it is sensible to wear a dust mask or prune on a wet day.

If you are handling plants that you know have caustic sap, such as euphorbia, wear gloves and long sleeves while you work.

The following plants are some of the more common ones that may cause problems. For further information consult the Royal Horticultural Society and the Horticultural Trades Association web sites:

Aesculus hippocastanum. Horse chestnut. The conkers and the leaves contain saponins.

Alstroemeria sp. Peruvian Lily. Can cause allergic reactions and blistering of the skin. This can be severe for people such as florists or flower packers who handle the plants regularly.

Borago officinalis. Borage. The hairy leaves and stems can cause rashes by abrasion. Worth growing for the star-like bright blue flowers which can decorate salads and Pimms.

Chrysanthemum sp. Handling the plants can cause severe skin irritation for some people.

xCuprocyparis leylandii. The Leyland cypress is often a problem for people during either pruning or trimming; besides producing a lot of dust that can cause coughing, the sap is a skin irritant.

Dieffenbachia. A house plant that is sometimes called Dumb Cane because if the sap gets into the mouth your tongue will swell and it becomes difficult to talk.

Elaeagnus ebbingei. Elaeagnus pungens. *Elaeagnus* is a tough evergreen plant with delicate flowers that give off a powerful scent. *E. pungens* has nasty thorns and can cause contact dermatitis and breathing problems.

Euphorbia pulcherrima. Poinsettia is usually sold near Christmas as festive decoration, but as with other *euphorbia* species, the sap can cause skin problems. They can cause vomiting and diarrhoea if ingested.

Ficus carica. Fig tree. The leaves and sap can cause skin allergies. If the sap is running when you are pruning, take care not to get it in your eyes. The decorative *Ficus* species may produce similar effects.

Fremontodendron californicum. California Glory. The leaves have tiny hairs that break off and get in your eyes, ears, mouth, nose and clothing. Not usually making you too ill but very unpleasant. Have a through wash, shower or bath and put clothes in the washing machine.

Hyacinthus sp. Handling the bulbs when selecting them and at planting can cause itchy rashes in some people. The bulbs contain 6 per cent of calcium oxalate crystals. Wear gloves to be on the safe side.

Hydrangea sp. If you grow hydrangeas, and one day you notice that somebody has cut off all the flower heads, do not be too surprised. It is not a case of senseless vandalism. It is a common occurrence on the European mainland since people discovered that you can get high by smoking the bracts of the flowers. As they contain cyanide like substances it is best not to try.

Lantana camara. Lantana is a shrub that has become more commonly available from garden centres in Britain. The plant is listed as an irritant and poisonous, especially the berries.

Nerium oleander. Oleander has been known as poisonous since Dioscorides. People have said to have been poisoned from using the branches as barbecue skewers.

Pastinaca sativa. Parsnips. Some people may have an allergic reaction to parsnip leaves and stems in bright sunlight, similar to rue and giant hogweed. There are reports of allergic reactions after eating parsnips.

Phlomis fruticosa. The hairs on the leaves can cause effects to hay fever. See *Fremontodendron*.

Rheum rhabarbarum. Rhubarb root was once used as a purge. Although used as a fruit, it is really a vegetable as it is the stalks that are eaten. The leaves should not be eaten because they contain oxalis acid.

Rhododendron sp. According to many sources, rhododendron can make you feel sick and nauseous; and some say that is from simply looking at them!

Rhus typhina. Stag's Horn Sumac. The sap can cause dermatitis or blistering. Poisonous.

Solanum tubersum. The potato contains solanine in the leaves, stems and fruits. The flowers are the most toxic part. Do not eat green potato tubers as they will contain more solanine than usual. It is best not to eat potatoes raw.

Symphoricarposalba. The Snowberry often grows in gardens and hedges close to habitation. Some books say that the white berries are safe to eat, but most say they are poisonous. As children, we squeezed the berries to make them make a noise- Pop!

Symphytum.sp. Comfrey is called knit-bone is some herbals and was used externally and internally for wounds. It is no longer recommended for internal use. The hairs can cause abrasive rashes.

Viburnum rhytidophyllum. A viburnum grown for its large, ribbed leaves. The stems and the back of the leaves produce very small hairs on the new growth. Do not prune this viburnum in July and August. The hairs break off and get in your eyes, nose and throat, producing a similar effect to a minor case of flu. The hairs can also cause rashes. I always prune it very early in the year. I certainly would not grow it myself; there are much better plants for the garden. Most web sites selling *Viburnum rhytidophyllum* do not mention this problem. See *Fremontodendron*.

Wisteria sp. The plant is toxic if ingested.

It is not only children you will need to be keeping an eye on in the garden; do not forget that many of the plants that are toxic to people are often toxic for your pets. It is easy to plant your own garden to be safe, but cats usually spend a lot of their time in somebody else's gardens too. Lily pollen can be of the greatest danger for cats. The pollen is often deposited on the cat's fur, the cat licks it off to clean itself and ingests the pollen.

There are numerous dangerous plants list for animals that can be found online.

https://www.woodgreen.org.uk/petadvice/
2793poisonousplantsandyourpet

https://www.dogstrust.org.uk/help-advice/factsheets-downloads/
factsheetpoisonoussubstances09.pdf

https://icatcare.org/advice/poisonous-plants

POISON GARDENS TO VISIT

There are few places that you can visit that specifically grow poisonous plants. Most Botanical Gardens will grow the plants of the same family in labelled beds or plants for specific uses in demonstration beds, medical or otherwise. Many gardens will be growing poisonous plants decoratively with no warning of the dangers.

ENGLAND
Alnwick Castle Poison Garden
Denwick Lane
Alnwick
Northumberland
NE66 1YU
Web site: https://alnwickgarden.com
Email: info@alnwickgarden.com
Telephone: 01665 511 350

Birmingham Botanical Gardens
Westbourne Road,
Edgbaston,
Birmingham
B15 3TR
Web Site: http://www.birminghambotanicalgardens.org.uk
Email: admin@birminghambotanicalgardens.org.uk
Telephone: 0121 454 1860

The Cambridge University Botanic Garden
1 Brookside
Cambridge
CB2 1JE
Web Site: http://www.botanic.cam.ac.uk/Botanic/Home.aspx
Email: enquiries@botanic.cam.ac.uk
Telephone: 01223 336265

The Chelsea Physic Garden
66 Royal Hospital Rd
Chelsea
London
SW3 4HS
Web Site: http://chelseaphysicgarden.co.uk/
Email: enquiries@chelseaphysicgarden.co.uk
Telephone: 020 7352 5646

The University of Oxford Botanic Garden,
Rose Lane,
Oxford
OX1 4AZ
Web Site: https://www.botanic-garden.ox.ac.uk
Email: admin@obg.ox.ac.uk
Telephone: 01865 286690.

Royal Botanic Gardens Kew
Richmond
Surrey
TW9 3AE
Web Site: http://www.kew.org
Email: info@kew.org
Telephone: 020 8332 5655

Torre Abbey
The Kings Drive
Torquay
Devon
TQ2 5JE
Web Site: http://www.torre-abbey.org.uk
Email: torreabbeyenquiries@torbay.gov.uk
Telephone: 01803 293 593

University of Leicester Botanic Garden & Attenborough Arboretum
Glebe Road
Oadby
LE2 2LD
Web Site: http://www2.le.ac.uk/institution/botanic-garden
Email: botanicgarden@le.ac.uk

WALES
The Botanic Garden of Wales
Middleton Hall
Llanarthne
Carmarthenshire
SA32 8HN
Web Site: https://botanicgarden.wales
Email:
Telephone: 01558 667 149

Bryngwyn Hall
Bwlch-y-Cibau
Llanfyllin
Powys
SY22 5LJ
Web Site: http://bryngwyn.com
Email: enquiries@brynwyn.com
Telephone: 01691 648647 or 07967 821191

Treborth Botanic Garden
Bangor University
Bangor, Gwynedd
Wales
LL57 2RQ
Web Site: http://treborth.bangor.ac.uk
Email: treborth@bangor.ac.uk
Telephone: 01248 353 398

SCOTLAND
Royal Botanic Garden Edinburgh
20A Inverleith Row
Edinburgh
EH3 5LR
United Kingdom
Web Site: http://www.rbge.org.uk
Email: visitorwelcome@rbge.org.uk
Telephone: 01315 527 171

NORTHERN IRELAND
Belfast Botanic Garden
Web Site: http://www.belfastcity.gov.uk/leisure/parks-openspaces/
Park-6614.aspx

EIRE
Blarney Castle
Web /site: http://www.blarneycastle.ie/pages/poison-garden
Email: info@blarneycastle.ie
Telephone: 00 353 21 438 5252

THE CONUNDRUM

We have come to the end of this book, and like many of the audiences that I have spoken to in the past, you have most likely forgotten all about Jane Austen's conundrum. So, as a reminder, here it is again.

'When my first is a task to a young girl of Spirit,
And my second confines her to finish the piece.
How hard is her fate, but how hard is her merit,
If by taking my whole she effects her release.'

If you have not guessed the answer and need a clue:
How did many Regency women pass their time productively?
She is confined - locked in.

The answer is - Hemlock.
The task for a young girl of spirit is to sew the hems on a piece of cloth. The second confines her to finish the piece, so she is locked in. Taking the whole is a rather drastic way to avoid doing her needlework.

A FINAL WORD

After the tales of death and poisons, do not let this put you off growing plants with toxic properties. I once read that eating too much cabbage could make you ill, although how much cabbage you would need to eat was not stated.

Children need to be educated as to what they can and cannot eat. My mother was told by her mother which plants were edible and which were not. My mother passed the information on to me. At some point in the 1970s, people seemed to lose contact with their surroundings and even this basic knowledge was not being passed on. Lack of knowledge can be dangerous.

There are surprisingly few cases of illness and death caused by accidental plant poisoning. The biggest problem is probably the misidentification of mushrooms, but foraging is becoming popular, so maybe the children of the future will once more know more about the plants that they can eat safely. Always double check any information that you receive whether from books, the internet or that given personally.

Finally, enjoy the plants for their beauty and the stories that have grown around them.

GLOSSARY

Alexipharmacon. An antidote to poison.

Allelopathy. A method whereby a plant can produce chemicals to affect the growth of neighbouring plants. Positive allelopathy assists the neighbours, whilst negative allelopathy restricts their growth and germination of kills the competitors.

Anaphrodisiac. A drug that suppresses sexual desire. The opposite of an aphrodisiac.

Anodyne. A medicine that relieves pain. It reduces the sensitivity of the nerves or brain. The term became obsolete by the twentieth century. Such drugs are now known as analgesics.

Anthelmintic. A medicine that kills or expels intestinal worms.

Aperient. A mild purge.

Apoplexy. An old name for what we now call a stroke.

Astringent. A medicine that causes the contraction of skin cells. Used to reduce bleeding or in cosmetics to help cleanse the skin and reduce the size of the pores.

Clyster. A medicine given as an enema.

Dioecious. A plant with male and female flowers on different plants.

Diuretic. A medicine that reduces the water content of the body, usually through urine.

Doctrine of Signatures. A system that followed the idea that God had very kindly made plants look like the diseases that they could cure. The spotty leaf of a *Pulmonaria* was supposed to appear similar to a diseased lung, so it would cure pulmonary disease. The botanical name *Pulmonaria* and the common name, Lungwort, both refer to the medicinal use of the plant.

Dropsy. An old term for the accumulation of water causing swelling in soft tissue. Modern medicine would define the specific cause, for example, oedema due to congestive heart failure.

Ectomycorrizal. Fungi that form a sheath around the root tip of the plant, a Hartig net, where the growth of fungus penetrates the plant root, to the mutual benefit of the fungus and the tree. The fungus receives organic elements and carbon from the tree and the tree is more able to take in water and minerals from the soil.

Elaiosome. A fleshy part that is attached to the seeds of some species of plants that attract insects, usually ants, to help with the dispersal of the seeds. The name comes from the Greek, *élaion* meaning oil and sóma meaning body.

Emmenagogue. A medicine that induces or increases the menstrual flow.

Epidermis. The outer cell layer of a plant; the equivalent of human skin.

Genus: Part of the binomial system of naming plants and animals. Many plants or animals may be part of the same genus, in a similar way as lots of people in a family have the same surname.

Monoecious. Plant species that carry male and female flowers on the same plant.

Myrmecochory. A method of seed dispersal through the use of ants; from the Greek for ant, *myrmex* and *kore* for dispersal.

Narcotic. A medicine that can induce sleep or relieve pain in small doses. In large doses it can affect the mind and behaviour. Now mostly used in reference to illegal drugs for recreational use.

Node. Plants have nodes on the roots and the stems. The stem node is a point where the leaf will grow from the stem; adventitious roots may also grow from the point, which is useful if you are taking cuttings. A root node is a similar point on the roots from which more roots may develop or a new stem may arise. A node usually shows as a bulge on the stem or root.

Purgative. A medicine that induces the evacuation of the intestines.

Quinsy. A Peritonsillar *abscess*. A swelling in the throat as a result of a severe complication of Tonsillitis, when pus develops next to the tonsil. It was known for patients to die within a day.

Rhizome. A modified subterranean stem of a plant, often sending out roots and shoots from its nodes to spread very quickly.

Sedative. A medicine that relieves pain and has a soothing, calming or tranquilising affect which can lead to sleep.

Soporific. A medicine that induces drowsiness or sleep.

Spadix. A fleshy spike-like flower stem that carries very tiny flowers. The spadix is often enclosed by a spathe. The Araceae family of plants is the most well known for having a spadix. The family includes, Anthurium, Arisaema, Arum, Spathiphyllum and Zantedeschia. Most are monoecious and have male flowers above the female ones.

Spathe. A bract that encloses a spadix. Many are coloured.

Vermifuge. A medicine that kills or expels intestinal worms.

ACKNOWLEDGMENTS

Thank you to the Oxford Botanical Garden and the Chelsea Physic Garden for allowing me to photograph some of the plants in this book. Most of the other plants were photographed at the Prebendal Manor Medieval Gardens at Nassington, which I designed and planted.

Thank you to Margaret for her help with editing and a special thank you to J for the encouragement to complete the book.

Picture Credits

The copyright to all the photographs in this book belong to the author, except for the following:

Doctor giving an enema: Cod. Sang. 760, f.120, St. Gallen, Stiftsbibliothek.

Drimia maritima: By Ziounclesi (Own work) [CC BY 3.0 (http://creativecommons.org/licenses/by/3.0)], via Wikimedia Commons.

Upas Tree: Wellcome Trust: V0019479ER Credit:Wellcome Library, London. Drunkards reaching for liquid falling from a deadly upas-tree. Coloured etching by G. Cruikshank, c. 1842, after himself.

Death in the Garden drawn by Kate Mills.

BIBLIOGRAPHY

ARDERNE, John. Ed. POWER, D'Arcy (ed):. *Treatises of 'Fistula in Ano' and of fistulae in other parts of the body and of apostumes making fistulae, and of and tenasmon, and of clysters haemorrhoid also of certain ointments, powders and oils.* The Early English Text Society. Oxford University Press.1968.

BARKER, Julian:. *The Medicinal Flora of Britain and Northwestern Europe.* Winter Press. 2001.

BEST, Michael R. Brightman (ed): *The Book of Secrets of Albertus Magnus. Of the Virtues of herbs, Stones and Certain Beasts, also a Book of the Marvels of the World.* Ed. Best, Michael R. Brightman, Frank H. Weiser Books. 2004.

BRODIN, Gösta (ed): *Agnus Castus, A Middle English Herbal.* Ed. Brodin, Gösta. Upsala. 1950.

BROOK, Richard:. *New Cycplopaedia of Botany and complete Bok of Herbs: forming a history and description of all Plants, British and Foreign.* Vols. I and II. W. M. Clark. Undated.

BROWN, Deni: *The Royal Horticultural Society Encyclopedia of Herbs & their Uses.* Brown, Deni. Dorling Kindersley. 1995.

CAKER, Margaret: *Discovering The Folklore of Plants.* Baker, Margaret. Shire Publications. 1999.

DARWIN, Erasmus: *The Botanic Garden: A poem, in Two Parts... the Economy of Vegetation, and the Loves of the Plants. With Philosophical Notes.* Darwin, Erasmus. Nabu Public Domain Reprints. 1825.

DAWSON, Warren R.: *A Leechbook or Collection of Medical Recipes of the Fifteenth Century. The text of s. No. 136 of the Medical Society of London, together with a transcript into modern spelling, transcribed and edited with an introduction, notes and appendix.* Dawson, Warren. R. MacMillan and Co., Limited, London. 1934.

FRISK, Gösta (ed): *Macer Floridus de Viribus Herbarum.* Ed. Frisk, Gösta. Upsala 1949.

GRAVES, Robert: *The White Goddess*. Graves, Robert. Faber and Faber Ltd. London. 1975.

GREEN, Monica H. (ed and trans): T*he Trotula. An English Translation of the Medieval Compendium of Women's Medicine*. Edited and translated by Green, Monica, H. University of Pennsylvania Press, 2002.

GRIEVE, M., LEVEL, C.F. (eds): *A Modern Herbal*. Grieve, M., Mrs. Ed. Leyel, C. F. Mrs. Merchant Book Company Ltd. Surrey. Originally printed 1931.

GRIGSON, Geoffrey *The Englishman's Flora*. Grigson, Geoffrey. Readers Union. Phoenix House. London. 1958.

GUNTHER. R. T:. *The Greek Herbal of Dioscorides*. Englished by John Goodyer A.D. 1655. Hafner Publishing Company. London and New York. 1968.

HINE, Florence: *A Chaplet of Herbs. Gatherings from the early Herbals*. Hine, Florence. George Routledge & Sons, Limited. London. No date. Poss.c. 1915.

HORT, Sir, Arthur. (trans), GOOLD, G. P. (ed): *Theophrastus. Enquiry into Plants. II*. Loeb Classical Library. Harvard University Press.1980.

HOZESKI, Bruce W.: *Hildegard's Healing Plants. From her medieval classic* 'Physica.' Hozeski, Bruce W. Beacon Press. 2001.

JOHNSON, Thomas: *Gerard's Herball. The Herball or Generall Historie of Plantes. Gathered by John Gerarde of London*. The Minerva Press Ltd. 1971.

LAWS, Bill: *Spade, Skirret and Parsnip*. Laws, Bill. Sutton Publishing.2004.

The Chemist and Druggist, London. 1946.

MARKHAM, Gervase: *The Whole Art of Husbandry Contained in Four Bookes*. Markham, Gervase. Captaine. 1631. EEBO Editions reprint.

PARKINSON, John: *A Garden of Pleasant Flowers. Paradisi in Sole Paradisus Terrestris*. Parkinson, John. 1629. Dover Publications. 1976.

PLINY: *Natural History. Books 20 -23*. Trans. Jones, W. H. S. Loeb Classical Library. Harvard University Press. 1999.

PLINY: *Natural History. Books 24 – 27*. Trans. Jones, W. H. S. Ed.

Henderson, Jeffrey. Loeb Classical Library. Harvard University Press. 2001.

PLINY: *Natural History. V. Books 17-19.* Trans. Rackham, H. Ed. Henderson, Jeffrey. H. Loeb Classical Library. Harvard University Press. 2004.

PLINY: *Natural History. With an English Translation in Ten volumes. IV. Books XII -XVI.* Trans. Rackham, H. Loeb Classical Library. Harvard University Press.1960.

PUGHE, John (trans)Esq., WILLIAMS ab Ithel, John (ed). *The Physicians of Myddfai; Meddygon Myddfai;* Trans. Facsimile reprint Llanerch Publishers, Felinfach. 1993.

RUDGLEY, Richard: *The Alchemy of Culture. Intoxicants in Society.* Rudgley, Richard. British Museum Press.1993.

STANNARD Jerry, STANNARD, Katherine. E. and KAY, Richard. (eds): *Herbs and Herbalism in the Middle Ages and Renaissance.* Ashgate Publishing Company. 1999.

STARÝ, Francis *Poisonous Plants.* Starý, Francis. Hamlyn. 1983.

STRABO, Walahfrid: *Hortulus.* Strabo, Walahfrid. Trans. Payne, Raef. Commentary. Blunt, Wilfrid. The Hunt Botanical Library, Pittsburgh. 1966.

TURNER, William: *Libellus de Re Herbaria. 1538. The Names of Herbes. 1548.* Turner, William. The Ray Society, London. 1965.

TUSSER, Thomas, *Five Hundred Points of Good Husbandry.* https://play.google.com/books/reader?id=6e41hIGwGcAC& printsec=frontcover&output=reader&hl=en_GB&pg=GBS.PA163

VAN ARSDALL, Anne: *Medieval Herbal Remedies. The Old Englsh Herbarium and Anglo-Saxon Medicine.* Routledge, New York and London.2002.

WILSON, C. Anne (ed): *The Country House Kitchen Garden 1600-1950.* Ed. C. Anne Wilson. Sutton Publishing Ltd. 2003.

WITHERING, William, *An account of the foxglove and some of its medical uses; with practical remarks on the dropsy, and some other diseases.* 1785
https://play.google.com/books/reader?id=2ElHAQAAMAAJ&printsec=
frontcover&output=reader&hl=en_GB&pg=GBS.PP5